Unders the Depressions

A Companion for Sufferers, Relatives and Counsellors

Wyn Bramley

First published by Free Association Books.

Copyright © 2020 Wyn Bramley

A CIP Catalogue of this book is available from
the British Library

ISBN: 978-1-91138-338-3

Typeset by
Typo•glyphix
www.typoglyphix.co.uk

Cover design by
Candescent

Printed and bound in England

Contents

Chapter 1

What *Are* "The Depressions"?

Out, out, brief candle
Life's but a walking shadow, a poor player,
That struts and frets his hour upon the stage,
And then is heard no more. It is a tale
Told by an idiot, full of sound and fury,
Signifying nothing

William Shakespeare (*Macbeth*)

We all share identical properties that mark us out as human beings. Even so, every person is unique: we are not clones. It's the same with depression – or perhaps more properly the depressions (plural) – because they manifest in so many different ways and under different circumstances yet in essence remain the same. This is a simple enough observation, yet there appears to be little understanding of the condition – or conditions – among the general public, who tend to lump together all states of "feeling miserable" into something to be snapped out of, a disease category to be treated medically, or a feebleness of personality to be disapproved of and dismissed.

To test this assumption I conducted some amateur research at my local pub and shopping centre. I asked random people of varying ages the simple question "What do you think it means when people say they're depressed?" Herewith a sample of replies: "It's feeling wretched most of the time", "a psychiatric illness", "suicidal?", "need to pull themselves together, stop feeling sorry for themselves", "off their trolley, no such thing", "just another excuse: get a life mate", "everybody's depressed, the state the world's in", "another way of saying very unhappy isn't it, sort of stuck in sadness?"

These answers do show how vaguely understood depression is, though all respondents connected it with a negative outlook and feeling low. There is ample, largely professional *knowledge* concerning depression, how it shows itself to the outward observer or physician; but there's very little *understanding* of what it actually feels like to be depressed (unless of course one suffers oneself). Perhaps folk have witnessed depression in others and fear contamination, though they know full well it isn't contagious. Perhaps they've felt that awful sense of impotence when one tries fruitlessly to cheer up the sufferer, talk them out of their misery; better to steer clear.

A car park interview

Okay, so what does this seemingly scary state that we label "depression" actually consist of? The first thing about it that we need to take very seriously is its complexity and its variety. I'm going to say a bit about Frank, a talkative Yorkshire man, and his personal experience of his wife's depression. This example shows how hard it is to simply seal off depression from its immediate context, as if it were an encapsulated thing like a growth that needs excising, or a bug that needs antibiotics. Depression transpires in a network of personal relationships – partners, kids, parents, work colleagues. It often destabilises the traditions, alliances, and problem-solving measures that have till now been the mainstay of the depressed person's family or work group. (Occasionally though, someone's depression grants an opportunity for all concerned to re-jig their shared relationships into a more wholesome way of operating. Some theorists claim that many depressions actually result from toxic family or workplace dynamics.) In trying to deal constructively with one's own depression or someone else's, this bigger picture has always to be taken into account if there is to be any benefit to those involved.

I met Frank at Tesco's checkout where we fell to chatting. Once outside I put my survey question to him. It was spitting with rain and to my surprise he pulled me by my arm toward the sheltered bit of the car park. He plonked down his shopping bags and turned eagerly toward my enquiring face. "Aye lass, I can tell you all about depression. You can stick this in your blinking book 'cause no one really gets it. Somebody should tell 'em."

"My wife has got it – real bad, takes all the tablets and that. Can't wake up in the morning till I pours three cups of strong tea down her, and even then she's woozy – from bad dreams she says. I gets the kids off to school and packs me own lunchbox and off I goes. I gets home from the plant totally knackered around half six – bloody awful traffic. All I wants is some grub, bit of telly and bed.

"Now the missus, she bucks up in the evenings since she's on them pills. Lipstick, cooks a nice meal, new frock. You know what she wants don't you? Well I can't. I'm a morning man in that department, alus was. So was she till she got depression. Then I gets tears, rage, doors banging. 'You don't love me anymore. You think I'm past it. I'm going to chuck that telly out the window!' Aye, she gets right hysterical. What am I supposed to do? One minute I have to play Nursey, the next a ruddy stud. We never have any of the old conjugals now, neither of us tries, only way to keep the peace. We barely speak to each other. I'm miserable, the kids are miserable. What about my depression eh? I don't get pills do I?"

Poor bloke didn't know which way to turn; he needed desperately to offload onto someone. His story clearly demonstrates how inadequate a solely chemical approach is to something as multi-factorial as depression. We don't know his wife's circumstances, though she seems to be as worried as he about the marriage and their sexual relations. Did these difficulties cause the depression, you might ask, or were they its result? Was the wife having side effects from the drugs? Was hubbie really too tired at night, or secretly resentful that the depression took his wife away from him in the mornings when he most needed her? He certainly saw the depression as the enemy, almost a rival.

What does it feel like?

As illustrated by this example, the sufferer's dark inner world inevitably impacts on their nearest and dearest. Relationships can be sorely tested. Sometimes the depressed person is only too aware of this, feeling increasingly guilty and self-reproachful. They try hard to disguise their mood until the effort becomes unsustainable and they collapse, to the surprise of others who had never suspected. In tragic cases suicide may prove the only escape from that Herculean effort of putting a good face on things, and the only way to protect family and friends from their "being a burden".

Depression is primarily a mood disturbance, rather than a thought or behaviour one. We all have mood signatures with which our friends and colleagues are familiar. Some even-tempered people's mood over time might be represented by a straight line. Others' moods could be drawn like a wave, rocking gently up and down. Still others are stormy, peaks and troughs in the wave, moving rapidly from optimism to pessimism, buoyant one minute, gloomy and despondent the next. These signatures vary almost as much as written ones on legal documents. So long as the mood signature of a person remains more or less constant, they may be said to be free of mood disorder. Should someone who usually swings in mood become flat as a straight line for a sustained period though, perhaps friends should worry rather than feel reassured that peace has broken out!

Depressed mood is something we all experience. According to the dictionary, one definition of depression is a "sunken hollow place" and on a bad day that's just what our whole organism – body, mind, and soul – feels like! This is a normal if unpleasant mood variation, which can occur without any especial stimulus, though often sad news, a bad decision or an unhappy event precedes it. Sometimes it will be worse and bother us for longer than usual. All the same, it runs its course before fading away and our characteristic mood sequence returns. This kind of temporary negativism is what we colloquially call depression but is *not* the subject of this book. This is not to minimise its importance, but it isn't what we are concerned with here. Colloquial depression is well within the bounds of normal mental health – we can't be happy all the time. However, any so-called depression that fails to resolve itself – becomes protracted, adversely affects otherwise good relationships, or causes the person to not enjoy their usual pleasures and interests – I'm going to mark as "little 'd'" from now on to make clear we are in new territory. The person knows something is going wrong; they are up against psychological distress beyond common unhappiness.

What about "big 'D'" then? I will use this to cover all those Depressions that without question require medical intervention on top of any other help; they have to be defined as an illness, whatever other crises may be simultaneously occurring. They often recur on a regular or irregular basis so that the sufferer comes to know and better manage the warning signs. At the deepest point in the Depression there is serious suicidal risk and the person may lose the ability to be objective about their condition. Nevertheless, as with little 'd', there are degrees of severity and over the course of any Depressive episode mood can lift or sink from day to day, sometimes hour to hour or moment to moment. A grey area exists between little 'd' and big 'D' and when referring to this, or making a comment on all Depressions collectively, I will use the big 'D'. I trust you'll soon get used to this.

While we are talking about nomenclature, you will also be introduced to the idea of a Self (capital S). We all have a picture of the kind of person we would like to show to the world, beautiful and clever perhaps, or caring, or adventurous, creative or successful. At the end of each day, should we review how our actual Self performed, we may find ourselves happy with it or critical of it, disappointed in it or angry with it. We have a relationship with our Self that obviously impacts on mood if we are always at loggerheads with it. I will discuss Self Psychology in a later chapter.

A Depression of whatever sort describes a *process* – not an infection or a growth you have either "got" or not got, as my Tesco man seemed to think. An astute observer or an experienced sufferer can trace its course as it deepens, gets stuck a while, then gradually or suddenly lightens. People undergoing regular or intermittent Depressions, as well as their relatives, carers and counsellors, can benefit from identifying each step of the route toward illness and afterwards toward recovery. The terrain along the way may be ghastly but at least you know where you are and what to expect.

When does little 'd' become a medical matter?

At what point can we say someone is actually ill? Usually we deem a person sick when they can't function well enough in their day to day relationships and job to "keep the show on the road". We call it a nervous breakdown. Our sympathies are mobilised. Depression is tricky however, because some sufferers inhabit two worlds at once. Shame, impossibly high standards, an over-developed sense of obligation or responsibility force some to carry on, whilst inside all is despair. From the outside they seem no different. So are they ill? Perhaps unhappiness becomes illness when a point is reached where pleasure in anything at all has become impossible (the text books call it *anhedonia*) and where hope has vanished from the horizon. Yet still some struggle on, keeping up appearances.

How it feels on the inside, not how it appears on the outside, is what in my view as a therapist defines the line that crosses into that domain where some kind of professional help is required. Many people who have to bear cyclical periods of this ailment, be this little or big 'D', know the oncoming signs so well ("Hello darkness my old friend" as the song goes) that they can identify the very second a lingering oppressive mood has become a Depression. One of my clients told me: "It's like someone sticking a seat belt on you. There's that noise in your head – clunk-click; you know with awful dread that you're now strapped in, but it's *trapped* in, really. No way out. You need help."

From the point of view of family or friends there may no evidence to explain such a loss of vitality and the complete inability to fight it. Parading the sufferer's achievements before them, listing the people who love them, urging them to think positive or look forward to their holiday is of no avail, for the mood state is now all-encompassing. The person can't be cheered up or consoled, for whilst they are affected (Depressions do end!) there is no belief that optimistic ways to view the world are possible. This loss of the capacity for hope *is* the illness. This is what non sufferers find so hard to grasp. For them hope springs eternal, even in the direst circumstances. Hope is a survival mechanism so rooted in our make-up that we cling to it even when the game is clearly up. If you want to understand the Depressions, try to imagine what it must be like to lose this life-line.

There's a huge discrepancy between how the sufferer sees the world *now*, and how they saw it when well. They may know that very well, but it makes not a jot of difference to them. Their negative perceptions feel like the truth to them, their previous "normality" an illusion. Arguing with them won't get you anywhere. *Reason makes no inroads into mood.* Look at someone who has just fallen in love, is over the moon. You can prove beyond doubt that their lover is a crook, a cheat and a liar, but does it affect their buoyant mood? As with the Depressions, you need to bide your time.

If a Depressed person can be persuaded to describe accurately their interior experience, the listener may be shocked by its extremity, may feel the narrator must be lying or exaggerating. They are not. Part of their mind is "out of order" like a faulty washing machine stuck on only one setting. Their reason is perfectly intact, but their mood unalterable, their optimism button jammed. Is it any wonder partners and pals feel powerless to help, or become irritated and critical of the sufferer who sometimes looks as if they are stubbornly refusing to cheer up? They can't cheer up. When the affected person's state is at its lowest ebb, that negative mindset is experienced by them as a permanent, pitiless reality: what conceivable point is there in trying? This is not stubbornness, which after all requires some effort, but hopelessness, which renders effort impossible.

Signs and symptoms

Let's now review the clinical symptoms in the Depressions, the kind of things diagnosing GPs are looking out for. Not all are evident in every case and some patients will present but a few. Usually, but not always, one feature dominates the rest. And we should be aware that little 'd' depression can slide in and out of big 'D' over a short or long time span, until it eventually becomes clear what kind of manifestation we are dealing with on a particular occasion. While this disordered (i.e. out of kilter with the usual) mood prevails, it's essential that GPs, relatives, friends and counsellors desist from poking and prodding it as if it were a thing, an inconvenient lump to be surgically cut away, medicated or radiated out of existence. The Depressed person is psychologically isolated enough already, without making things worse by prioritising their symptoms over their person.

Medical considerations are only one among many when trying to help. My Tesco man was already edging toward small 'd' himself, because no one recognised his problems, and he looked likely to deteriorate. At the same time his wife was improving biochemically but was left to deal with the consequent sexual issues without aid. This couple received but crude and superficial assistance, the interpersonal dimension in the Depressions excluded entirely from the treatment plan – if there was a treatment plan! I will look at available physical and psychological treatments, with stories from those who underwent them, in a later chapter.

There are many physical manifestations of the Depressions, but they usually assert themselves first as a psychological disruption. The individual's self-damning attitudes to, and negative judgements of, their own person are out of character. (It has to be admitted though, that some normally gloomy characters become Depressed and no one notices, due to the lack of contrast between their well mood and their gradually disordered one.) There is usually a pervasive aura of sadness and/or defeatism about the individual, or less commonly they emanate a smouldering rage against a cruel world. Typically the episode will have a distinct beginning, middle and end, and each phase may be fast or slow. Distorted, disproportionate, overly pessimistic beliefs and self-critical judgements flow from the low mood, gaining force or dissipating according to whether the episode is progressing or receding. All the same, recovery can be far from linear and tidy: two steps forward, one step back, is more common. In assessing any type of Depressive episode – what to do about it, when and how – the idea of time, the concept of ebb and flow, is of central importance.

In any helping role one needs and wants the collaboration of the sufferer. But if the mind that is out of order hates its own existence, can't believe in the possibility of healing, will not or cannot ally with the helper, what can the helper do? Hard though it will prove, maybe they can learn how to wait and discreetly watch, keep the person safe, fed and watered, while trusting that a better time will come, when they will be allowed in.

Many sufferers, counsellors, relatives and carers will recognise the following picture of middling to big 'D'. There is in addition to or in combination with the above, more pronounced self-loathing, excessive and unfounded guilt, overwhelming sensations of pointlessness, fatigue, even exhaustion. There can be emotional numbness or excessive irritability, inexplicable tears and/or regular involuntary sighing. The entire world may be perceived as irredeemably evil. This pervasive mood *can't be dislodged by any amount of rational argument, reassurance or proof that their mental state is inaccurate.* The individual concerned often knows with their intellect that the way they are experiencing the world is unbalanced, that by all accounts they are perfectly successful, the world a wonderful as well as disaster-ridden place, that they have committed no major crime, and so on; but the internal atmosphere remains unchanged. Their chemistry, whether cause or effect of their mood, is instructing their evaluating brain to operate as if these delusional ideas were true.

On the other hand, as we all know from the news, there are at the farthest end of the Depression spectrum those people who have lost touch with reality altogether (are psychotic) and who tragically kill themselves and their families in a loving but misguided attempt to protect them from an uncaring world. This mercifully rare form of Depression differs from other psychoses such as mania or the schizophrenias in that the person may seem outwardly normal and so their illness goes undetected until disaster strikes.

Mixed pictures and the importance of assessment

Neither does a Depression of any kind inoculate you against other conditions. People who suffer anxiety or panic attacks can experience all the signs of a Depression, from the mildest to the most severe, with or without their usual symptoms being present. People with controlled eating disorders, chronic migraines, ongoing marital and family issues, addiction, post-traumatic stress, and learning difficulties can become both little 'd' and big 'D' affected, sometimes together with, but often quite independently of, their usual complaints. The new situation requires fresh investigation, but is frequently missed by counsellors and medics concentrating on the old familiar picture, as if, once labelled, their client was unchangeable.

Assessment is a delicate matter calling for time and skill. Separately *or* combined with other markers, the Depressions can feature in many other disorders – schizophrenia for instance, where thinking and perception (hearing voices, believing one is being spied on and so forth) dominate. The one set of symptoms doesn't cancel out the other, but are they related, reinforcing one another? Or are we dealing with two distinct entities with different origins, perhaps requiring different management?

Similarly, social isolation and loneliness, especially in old age, can descend into one of the Depressions without anyone noticing. Loneliness creates the conditions for rumination, the surfacing of regrets, the missing of dead partners and friends. This "ordinary" colloquial depression may be tolerated till one day the sufferer appears in the GP's surgery unable to carry on. Common unhappiness without neighbourly or family input easily degenerates into little 'd' or even, if neglected long enough, big 'D' Depression. Ever receding realistic hope of companionship leading to inner desolation is the main culprit here.

In summary then, symptoms of Depression may disguise other disorders or relationship problems that, once correctly diagnosed and attended to, can relieve the Depression symptoms quickly, or prevent little 'd' form turning into the big one! I will share real examples in future chapters.

The prescription pad may be very useful as part of a helping plan, but should not be pounced on as if it were a cure-all. A careful assessment needs to be made before any action is taken: family history, recent exacerbating or contributory life events, the current state of the subject's personal relationships, their internal preoccupations, dreams, levels of pessimism, their eating and sleeping, plus reported or observed signs of physical slowing down. All these factors have a bearing on the Depressions. A thorough appreciation of any episode's genesis, whether it stands alone or is part of a mix, whether it replicates or deviates from previous ones, can go some way toward preventing or better treating a further attack.

Counselling and psychotherapy

Counselling and psychotherapy have much to offer, if accessed at the right time and with the individual's un-coerced agreement. If, for the moment, they are too drugged and woozy, or too lacking in hope to collaborate, it will be wiser to wait till any antidepressants have had some effect, so that the person's mood is lifted just sufficiently for them to be able, however doubtfully, to take an interest in their own recovery. For another perceived failure could confirm their worst fears about themself, tear up their last shred of self-esteem. Marching them before a therapist may temporarily reassure the scared relative or partner, but could jeopardise or squander a future invaluable resource. Patience and tact are needful. Sadly there is no magic "cure" for all the Depressions or for the understandable anxiety and frustration of loved ones.

With help, those unfortunate enough to endure recurrent bouts of this malaise can come to recognise how their unique Depression operates – its personality so to speak. They know from experience it will come again, so they "do a deal" with it rather than fighting a war they can't win. Alleviation strategies are at the ready, including drugs or not, depending on what has helped in the past. They find a philosophical outlook that enables them to live alongside it, much as malaria sufferers have to put up with relapses but refuse to let them contaminate other aspects of their life, the ones they so enjoy when well. The restless (and depressing!) search for a total "cure" is exchanged for a degree of grudging acceptance. With the help of wise counsel from someone who truly understands their private hell, they can develop ways of existing with, rather than raging against or totally surrendering to, this unwelcome visitor.

A one-off incident in a *non*-regular sufferer can sometimes be cleared up for good, once the antecedents are traced and come to terms with. Many episodes function like anaesthetic, numbing painful memories or traumas from the past that are threatening to re-emerge into consciousness. Often a marriage, a death, becoming a parent, divorcing, losing a job, triggers the mobilisation of long buried but unresolved historical issues. This delicate and deep work takes a professional skill that goes further than empathy and support. I will share true but anonymised stories about such therapeutic intervention in later chapters.

Counsellors and psychotherapists regard little 'd's and big 'D's as disordered mood states of the whole organism, not just some sequestered mental abnormality. Mind and body is one interrelated system. If you dissect a human corpse you'll not find the mind anywhere. It's an artifice, a construct that we deploy for the purposes of communicating with each other about our interior experiences. The body would be no more than a sophisticated robot without a mind, and the mind can't come to life without the incorporated brain and its essential chemical, hormonal and electrical supplies. It's for linguistic convenience only that we talk about the "mind" affecting the "body" and the "body" affecting the "mind", for they are one and the same. We describe how these notionally separate units speak for one another, but really the whole organism is speaking for itself. The "mind" registers embarrassment, the physical face blushes. The student's "mind" is saturated with anxiety as the exam paper is opened, but simultaneously their pulse races, their armpits stream with sweat, their heart thumps. The "physical" pain after the same surgical operation is experienced differently by different patients – requires more or less morphine – depending on their "mental" attitude to pain.

Whilst exploring quite other emotional or relationship matters with a client, the therapist is always on the look-out for signs that their client may be slowing down. Where there is persistent low mood, blood flow is sluggish, the skin pale; muscles don't want to flex, there's listlessness; digestion seems to stop and there are grumbles about constipation. The client reports that recently just lifting a kettle to make tea feels like carrying a boulder. Walking through the kitchen is wading through treacle. Lassitude makes the person crave their duvet, or alternatively dread and anxiety accompany all attempts at sleep. Recounting these changes as if they were oddities of little consequence, and preoccupied with other relationship worries, the client often fails to realise they are becoming Depressed. It falls to the therapist to remedy the situation.

Internal conflict in the Depressions

Internal conflict (opposing wishes and desires that are irreconcilable), both conscious and unconscious, is commonly associated with little 'd', and sometimes triggers a major Depressive episode in someone vulnerable to these. However conflict is not an absolute requirement for the diagnosis. As mentioned above, the loss of hope may come about through purely social causes, or multiple bereavements too overwhelming to absorb, or terminal illness that can't be come to terms with. Some people are constitutionally susceptible to low mood, so that even small setbacks in their lives evaporate what little hope they normally entertain. The elements that make up a person's constitution and how these might contribute toward the Depressions will be discussed in chapter two. Still, internal conflict demanding the anaesthesia of Depression is so frequent that it necessitates illustration.

Philip's conflicts, conscious and hidden

Philip, fifty-six, unmarried, had always had a poor relationship with his Self. When he looked in the mirror he'd always seen a weedy sort of specimen, uninteresting, just about able to manage his lowly admin job and the house he shared with his widowed mother. A year ago she'd been diagnosed with Alzheimer's and was going downhill quite quickly. There were no other surviving family members so his life appeared mapped out for the foreseeable future.

Then he met a lady chef in the canteen at work. She was also single, living alone in a bedsit. She had ailing parents in Ukraine, looked after by her bothers, to whom she was promised to return when her visa ran out in six months' time. They both seized this last chance opportunity for happiness, shyly enjoying several months of courtship before Katya's departure date loomed. She begged him to go home with her.

He couldn't bear to put his mother in a nursing home though he longed to leave England and start a new, more optimistic life. He had for the first time encountered happiness, fulfilment, and he was already nearly sixty. He'd never in his life taken risks, put himself first. Surely he could allow himself this chance? Mum would need constant care soon in any case, so why not leave now? But she had looked after him all his lonely, under-confident life; how could he desert her now? The constant guilt and indecisiveness grew unbearable, and a few weeks before Katya was due to return home he suddenly sank into a torpor, uncommunicative, overcome with a sadness so immobilising and heavy he was unable to go to work. Despite her dementia, his mother in her more lucid periods, and Katya too, saw his decline and insisted he see someone.

It's obvious why such a dilemma might make someone in Philip's position very miserable, but did that warrant a complete shutdown? Why did he succumb to so dangerous an illness? The answer lies in an internal conflict of which Philip was completely ignorant until he commenced therapy and talked at length about his much loved mother.

Philip always emphasised his mother's reliance on and need of him, as her only son; but in fact there had been another son, unexpectedly stillborn, whose name had already been chosen – Philip. The Philip described here was conceived very soon after and the dead infant never spoken of again. Philip learned of the baby by accident, overhearing his gran and a neighbour at the garden fence, so his questions had had to be answered. He couldn't remember what his reaction had been at the time, but till now he'd assumed it was all forgotten, that life had just gone on as usual. He'd never introspected much and had always believed his childhood to have been rather dull, but happy enough. The only odd thing was that around each birthday he'd always felt unaccountably sad, never enjoyed his parties or presents much. He'd shrugged this off as "just one of those things".

Over time in therapy we were able to reconstruct his forgotten childhood conflict, long buried but stirred up again by the new conflict over Katya and his mother. His young mind had decided that he must never enjoy life too much, never take centre stage and expect attention, never be too successful, or seek praise. For all these prizes would have been won at the expense of the child to whom they really belonged and who was denied any pleasure in them. His life had been purchased at the cost of his brother's death. He could only justify his existence by comforting his mother for her terrible loss; that was his lifelong role if he was to avoid guilt and punishment for relishing life while his brother could not.

His late blooming love for Katya had dared him at last to defy brother and mother and for the first time live on his own terms in a new country (literally and metaphorically). He experienced a sense of wild liberation at the prospect, but in response to it an immediate guilt-soaked self-hatred that was so awful that both leaving and staying tortured him equally. He could live with neither option and sank into hopeless inertia.

Philip recognised at once – "like a light bulb going on" – this picture of himself standing in the shoes of his dead brother, taking on a massive responsibility that was never really his, with the result that he could never claim his life as his own. As the dead baby ceased to haunt him and he accepted he could not do his mother's mourning for her, his mood lifted, along with his capacity to deal with the current conflict and its practical implications.

The couple decided they could not abandon their parents and parted, on the understanding that they would visit one another at Christmas, Easter and summer until nursing homes and/or parental deaths allowed them to be together. I don't know if the commuting relationship survived, but Philip was now so eager to make up for lost time that I suspect he made sure that it did.

A summary of this chapter

The Depressions come in various types and in varying degrees. One can be a bit down but able to hide it (common unhappiness), down for a longer period and only able to function like a zombie (little 'd'), or ill, sometimes so ill as to find life not worth the living (big 'D'). They differ from periods of unhappiness which, though extremely painful, are usually connected with adverse *external* circumstances – war, cancer, divorce – that the person believes will one day resolve. However far into the future, no matter how long the tunnel, there will be light at the end of it. It is this hope, no matter how unrealistic, that keeps us all going. At the lowest point in a Depression there is nothing to wait *for*. Make no mistake: the sufferer is not swallowed up by self-pity, but by a dark *internal* universe that's blind to hope.

Whatever its size, shape and duration, the disorder is not self-induced nor evidence of a weak personality. In World War I many soldiers were shot for showing signs of what we would nowadays call Depression. They were labelled cowards, traitors, nutcases, malingerers. Lack of backbone was supposedly the basis for symptoms, not causes beyond the soldiers' conscious control (you do not – cannot – decide or un-decide to be Depressed). Churchill was a pretty brave chap and we all know that he intermittently succumbed to what he called his "Black Dog".

The inter-related causes for the Depressions will be examined in the next chapter, though they remain unproven, inexactly measured and argued over, despite the most advanced research. My version of them arises more from clinical experience than academic research, though its general tenor would not be disputed by most professionals in the field.

Chapter 2

What Causes "The Depressions"?

Who falls prey to them and why? Are they inherited or acquired? Are they associated with intelligence, social or educational factors? Are certain personalities – artists, ambitious types, grumpy characters maybe – more susceptible than others?

The short answer is that there appears to be no isolated single determinant, except perhaps in the cases of severe and recurrent Depression or bipolar illness, where a personal and/or pronounced family history make clear that genes must dominate, whatever other factors may be involved. When, how and why those genetic tendencies become actualities, however, begs further research. Are incidents already primed to "go off" no matter what, like an alarm clock; or might there be predictors that, once identified, could mitigate an attack, or alert us sooner to an impending one?

Neither do profiles exist, boxes of personal characteristics to tick, that will neatly slot you into the different *types* of Depression you are likely to suffer, though there are indices, likelihoods. These types (chapters 4 and 5) are in any case sketches not portraits. Anyone of any intelligence, personality or background, whatever their genes, can be affected by mood disorder. Though adverse circumstances such as bereavement, poverty, redundancy might contribute to or worsen an already negative outlook, they're not single explanatory causes. The picture is more complex than that.

It may be more useful to look at the Depressions – from the littlest 'd' to the biggest 'D' – from a *dynamic* rather than a causative point of view, the word dynamism referring to a field of interplaying forces. A simple diagram can illustrate how many features within and without the individual can interact with each other in countless combinations and in constant movement to produce the state of mind (and body!) we know as Depression. The symptoms themselves will vary, wax and wane, according to the unique distribution of those features and which of them are being stimulated, charged if you like, in that especial person at a specific point in time. "Causes" are lifeless, abstract things: this diagram illustrates potent *forces* that move around in a person all the time, hence the possibilities for getting worse and (hallelujah!) for getting better.

The Human Onion

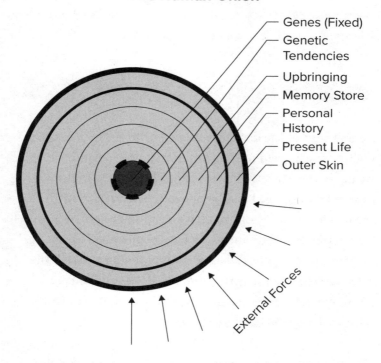

Genes (Fixed)
Genetic Tendencies
Upbringing
Memory Store
Personal History
Present Life
Outer Skin

External Forces

Think of a human being as an onion. There's a sturdy outer covering and vulnerable layers within. Not very poetic I know, but the analogy suits, because the human being and the onion are structured in a similar way. Should you peel back the "face" that a person shows to the world you will find layer upon layer of complex individual qualities behind it, be they deeply hidden or open for inspection, that have resulted from their unique life experience. Like the onion, each of those layers has an interconnected growth history. Possibilities still exist for them to grow, remain static or fade away. Let me now try to guide us through the main layers. Of necessity the diagram is two dimensional but try to keep in mind a real, spherical onion.

Genes

We will start at the densely wrapped centre. There's not much that will yield to pressure or that will expand or shrink, in the way other layers can. This core is analogous to your set of genes. Long before your brain has even finished forming, before you have anything remotely akin to a personality, your ancestors have bequeathed to you in the form of your genes a bag of both potential and definite characteristics. Some can't be changed – eye colour, left handedness, fingerprints. In the diagram these are represented by the blocked out centre.

You also inherit predispositions as well as certainties. For instance, a *tendency* toward anxiety, aggression, optimism or pessimism may lie within your genes, but it doesn't necessarily morph into mental illness. It all depends on whether life's vicissitudes draw out and reinforce the tendency or minimise the need to manifest it. These potentials surrounding the core are drawn as broken lines, just as in a real onion the deep embryonic shoots encasing the core can develop over time into a recognisable functioning layer or remain stunted, depending on growing conditions within and without the plant.

Upbringing 1
The nature/nurture debate

Having started at the centre of the diagram, we now work outwards, coming next to the huge area inside you that encompasses your upbringing; or rather, what you made of how you were brought up. For you participated in that process, had to somehow grow an identity out of it. You had to discover or decide who you were, how you were going to operate successfully within the universe of your family. You had to work out, albeit without consciously articulating it, whether and how to compete, share, declare a need, attack or defend yourself; whether and when your relationship with others in your home was best cultivated and enjoyed, and when it might be better avoided. Was your family experienced as safe and dependable or too emotionally threatening? Did it feel too close or too distant? Against this context, how difficult or easy did it feel to take pride in your strengths and achievements, or did you decide to hide or even reject them? Did you express your interests and pleasures or did you have to defend them against perceived saboteurs? All this work, *your* work, shaped your unique personality. It wasn't dropped into your head ready formed.

So far, no one has been able to accurately calculate what proportions of family and genetic influence go to make up both the mentally healthy and unhealthy person, though clinical experience places enormous weight on how a child interacts with its carers. Here's an example. Someone brought up in a violent household becomes violent too. Grandma on one side of the family is violent as well, but Granddad on the other is pious and withdrawn. Our violent person's equally abused brother or sister turns out to be gentle as the proverbial dove. How much is genes and how much upbringing? Were brother and sister's differing temperaments already sealed in by their genetic endowment, each having inherited different bits from the gene pool? Or were they fashioned from the disparate way each understood, reacted to and managed their relationships within the family? Common sense suggests there are complex combinations of Nature and Nurture operating here that can't be judged by simple arithmetic.

We should also remember that we inherit "positive" tendencies too: curiosity, optimism, gregariousness for instance (though these can work as much against us as for us, depending on how we deploy them). Some of these qualities may offset or compensate for the "negatives", but at birth all exist as merely potential, not actual, characteristics of the developing individual. They lie dormant. They are yet to be shaped by lived experience (upbringing) and of course the later learning/ unlearning/relearning process. Some children engage eagerly in learning about relationships whilst some are too sluggish and afraid to experiment – early conditioning or genetic predestination? Research cannot yet accurately quantify or map these determinants. We can only rely on educated guesses accrued from long clinical experience.

Upbringing 2
The consequences: relations with your Self

Your attitude to your own Self has a bearing on mood. The more you like, enjoy, feel proud of your own Self, the more your mood will hold up, whatever is occurring in your life. The more you doubt, disapprove of, are ashamed of your Self, the more readily undermined will be your mood. You can *act* confident, unafraid, anxiety free, but acting doesn't make it so. If you have a pretty unfavourable secret attitude to and beliefs about your own worth and attractiveness to others, you're clearly vulnerable when something bad happens. A job loss or ending of a relationship may confirm long held suspicions that you are a hopeless failure, that it must be your fault, and your mood collapses. Lack of self-esteem is learned, not genetic, and is a huge risk factor for many. It has to have arisen from early family "messages", overt or unspoken, deliberate or not, sent to you and absorbed by you as a child, aided and abetted by your self-critical interpretations of them. But don't forget that messages can to some extent be decoded and rewritten later on.

What is it then, that determines which of three people who lose their job becomes a) merely unhappy, b) little 'd' depressed, and c) big 'D' Depressed? The one who reacts with ordinary unhappiness is the one who, in the struggle we all go through to manage and learn from the early interpersonal forces around us, has grown a sense of Self that's sturdy enough to withstand minor knocks. On being dismissed – a rather big knock – they're disappointed, angry; they may be tearful, may shout at their partner, get drunk and maudlin, temporarily doubt their abilities. But there's no black cloud of self-loathing, no click clunk of that seat belt trapping them in forever. They don't hear hope scuttling away into infinity. (These descriptions are not inventions, hyperbole. They are how Depressed people really experience their temporarily disordered mood.)

The second person's usual relations with their Self aren't that good, due to early experiences where affirmation and encouragement were absent or where there were many separations from the family. They try to bolster their wavering self-esteem by being competent and dependable at work. Outward reassurance of their worth makes up for the lack of it inside. If that individual's personality is also genetically loaded with a proneness to low mood and then they are sacked, it's likely they'll become small 'd' depressed.

If our third person is also self-doubting and under confident, whilst being genetically subject to big 'D' from time to time, this job loss risks triggering another period of their illness. We still don't know to what degree, if any, a secure childhood reduces the likelihood of relapse or recurrence in big 'D' depression.

We may not be able to alter our genes, but quality therapy

can certainly help with issues of poor or negative regard for our Self, thereby increasing our resilience to Depression. There are no fast fixes in this area, despite many false assurances to the contrary. Tracing your own development, looking through a more adult and compassionate lens at those early formative years, can be as painful as it is illuminating. But for many, such a demanding project proves healing and mood-lifting in the end. Many derive emotional nourishment from their counselling encounter, of a quality rarely if ever received as a child, providing a miniature model of what good relationships outside the counselling room could be. As hope walks in, low mood walks out, though there may still be much work to do.

The Memory Store

Progressing outward from the deep core of our onion, through the area of upbringing, we next come to the memory store. As we have seen, our temperament has some genetic basis though the experts aren't sure yet to what degree. This is over-layered by the effects upon us of all those early relationships in the family (or other unit) that drew out, inhibited or even created a counterweight to those built-in propensities. We can't change what happened or failed to happen. We can't put the clock back, re-configure our very origins, though with therapeutic help we might learn to make peace with our early history. As we grew up we accumulated a rich chronicle of memories, documenting the vast amount of day to day interactions between ourself and our early attachment figures. Many of those memories and the feelings associated with them faded, whilst others were laid to rest yet refused to disappear completely. As we shall see, some were deeply buried, but proved capable of resurrection given auspicious circumstances.

Also recorded in our memory store are subsequent influential relationships with teachers, relatives, club leaders, tutors, and of course lovers and close friends. These newer figures functioned as moderators, reinforcers, growth or destruction agents for the already established but still adapting Self. Our emotional ties with these significant people profoundly affected the way we perceived and evaluated that Self, allowing it to further develop, repair old wounds even, or in sad cases to shrink into the shadows.

Though genes may impose some limitations, it's relations with others, good and bad, past and present, that determine whether or not we are in good odour with our Self, and hence how vulnerable we might be to mood imbalance. Because we are a living organism, our capabilities are always available for expansion or fine-tuning as well as injury and deterioration. Thus our relational abilities – to ourselves and to others – have a future as well as a past and the one does not *have* to repeat the other. This hopeful belief is what brings many into counselling, or into becoming counsellors themselves.

We are usually too busy or too wary to wander about the memory store, but its contents can unexpectedly jump out at us, more than once and in completely different settings. In thinking about memory in relation to the Depressions, I'm not referring to nostalgia, reminiscences, photo album memories, to be taken out and enjoyed. Rather do I mean scraps of long forgotten conversations, barely registered at the time. Or they could be complete mini-dramas suddenly recalled as they are eerily repeated in the present. A musical refrain from a distant radio might flood the unprepared mind with the memory of an entire relationship; not so much actual events as the conflicting, unresolved feelings linked to that attachment. A cupboard in a friend's kitchen unaccountably disturbs, till one day the wood grain is recognised as similar to a father's coffin twenty years ago. This then is a secret store, the memories not normally sought, or even retrievable, though in therapy some are more retrievable than others. Many memories are themselves beyond recall but the pain, anxiety or sensitivity connected to them remain in that store, and are provoked once more in certain present circumstances, as I show below.

Which comes first? Does heavy mood pile up outside the door of the memory store, eventually so weakening it that memories leak out? Or are those memories so powerful that they fight against their confines and erupt into awareness given the least opportunity, so precipitating low mood? For if memories have been put to sleep, locked away, surely they must be upsetting ones, capable of wounding the Self? As with the nature versus nurture debate we can't know for sure; we can only make educated guesses on a case by case basis. Here is an example from my own life. Did the lingering effects of my past, safely stored away for decades, determine the way I handled the present moment, or did the current situation so re-enact the past that my memory store's security was abruptly breached? Either way, a short little 'd' depression followed.

A marital row

My partner called into the pub for "a quick drink" after a tough day at work, there to bump into two old mates. He returned home hours later, just as I was considering phoning the hospitals. Not being a self-pitying cry-baby, I turned my hurt feelings into rightful indignation and yelled at him for being so selfish and unfeeling. He hadn't even let me know he was delayed. A trifle worse for wear and looking tired, he ignored my tirade and settled himself on the sofa. I was not going to get an apology. I went for him again: "Stop ignoring me! Honestly, you're heartless. I could be lying unconscious and bleeding on the pavement and you'd just step over me!" He looked up wearily, reached for the remote, clicked, and said "Don't be such a bloody drama queen". I was taken a-back, felt he'd switched me *off* as he switched the TV *on*. I was overcome with such sudden and extreme distress I feared physical collapse and staggered up to bed.

For the next few days I carried on as usual, but no matter how I tried I couldn't rid myself of an all-pervasive black mood. It felt as if the earth's atmosphere was being pressed down by a pall of ever thickening soot, no light or movement anywhere. I had to push myself to do anything, had to drag myself out of bed in the mornings. If this was some reaction to the row, it was totally out of proportion, and anyway we had by now talked all that through. What on earth was happening to me?

Then one night I was jolted awake, presumably by some dream. There was a little girl, still as a statue, staring out of our bedroom window bathed in brilliant, unnatural light. I shook my head – a momentary hallucination – before it, she, vanished. With the ease and practice of long habit, I fell to free associating (letting one thought and emotion drift around and eventually link itself to another). I was finally able to piece together what it was that had escaped my memory store to overwhelm me at the end of that row.

I began with the child at the window. Could she be me? She looked about five or six, pigtails. I had pigtails. The light, what about that strange light . . . ?

As a child I was extremely curious about and sensitive to the world about me, the physical as much as the interpersonal. I had intense emotional reactions to animals, people, nature. Ideas in themselves fascinated me; where did they come from? I asked endless questions which no one seemed able to answer. Everyone decided I was "highly strung" and I was teased about it frequently. I felt a freak, but if it kept them happy. . .

Around five or six years old, I woke one morning to find the world a fairyland of snow and ice – the real thing, deep and crisp and even, glistening and twinkling in bright sunlight. I was entranced, spent the entire morning at the window gazing out at it. I stood very still, afraid that to move or breathe might disturb this vision of loveliness that I was encountering for the first time. Mum kept calling me away but gave up in the end.

Finally we were called to the table to eat. I tore myself from paradise, to find myself literally blind! I screamed for help while Mum fiddled with pans and plates. I screamed again: "I can't *see!*" Continuing to serve up, mum said crossly "It's just the snow. Stop being so highly strung about it." I was terrified, had never heard of snow blindness, and assumed it was permanent. And no one seemed to care! Panic stricken, I protested but was sent to my room to lie down in the dark, purportedly to cure me, but I knew I was not believed (*I was being a drama queen*).

My terror in that dark room was twofold; one that I might never see again so could not survive alone, and two that my adored mother whom I trusted totally and on whom my whole life depended *did not believe me*. She had not calmed and comforted me: instead she'd mocked and scolded, sent me stumbling blindly to my room. I was utterly alone, cast out, and everyone thought I was just making it up. How could such things be possible? Without my mum, centre of my universe, there was no hope of rescue. The world was now as black inside as it was outside. I could only conclude that I had failed her in some monstrous way, let her down. It could not be down to her: she, the embodiment of perfection. The whole thing must be my fault *for being highly strung.*

It never occurred to me then that there might have been a failure of empathy on her part – *or on my husband's* when the ten o'clock news proved more important than my feelings of abandonment when he was so late. Once again I was condemned for being highly strung, a drama queen. The pain was unbearable. Was I never to be forgiven?

My sight gradually recovered over the next couple of days, but my faith in my previously sainted mother, and the husbands for whom she was the template, did not. Hence my rage at the casual lateness that had started the row in the first place.

Would the acute Depression have happened had my husband been more understanding or said he was sorry for causing me distress? Was it healing of an old wound that I was looking for, not a grovelling apology, as he'd assumed? Or were my memories associated with the snow blindness

– being banished, *extinguished* – just looking for an excuse to burst out? Was I yelling at my mother – "Understand me! Rescue me! Believe me!" – as much as at my husband? Staying late at the pub certainly provided a golden opportunity for such a re-enactment to occur.

Perhaps without knowing it I had hoped for a better outcome this time, and when I didn't get it the old despair took over. Whichever way round it was, I could now see the join-up between present and past. Having come to an understanding of my acute little 'd', I gave that poor kid a great big hug before leaving her behind.

Personal History

Look at the diagram again. As year by year you grow into your teens, then young adulthood, your genetic propensities (dotted line) combine with your early formative experiences plus that acquired memory store and its effects on you, to shape what sort of decisions and relationships you are going to persevere with and which ones you will let go of. Accordingly a unique personal history accumulates. Your educational and job choices, love affairs, how you spend your money, whether and where you travel, what hobbies you adopt, will all be largely determined by those background factors. They're not down to mere chance. You continue building up a unique history, a set of attitudes, aspirations, fears and so forth that will shape the outcome whenever you have to choose a direction, major or minor, along life's journey.

Whilst your memory store is relegated to the past, its contents kept behind closed doors, this Personal History layer is always readily available to you (unless you suppress it). It's a chronicle comprising your mistakes and successes; situations you ran from or faced; situations that you learned from or let hurt you, that you never want to encounter again or can't wait to have a re-run of and do it better this time. The items in this your personal file mould your dreams of a future way of life. You will seek something already designed in your head as a result of your historical choices and reactions to events. You will draw yourself a picture of just what kind of life in the future is going to make you happy, and which kind you wish at all costs to avoid.

As a young adult, more experienced and reflective, you may recognise some uncomfortable patterns in that history. When you look back, you see how some modes of relating or behaving kept repeating, bringing about unwanted consequences, despite your feeling good about other areas of your life. Perhaps you seek help to investigate their origins. The insight so gained enables you not only to straighten out some things but also to sharpen up the picture of how you want to live and relate to others in the next period of your life, how you visualise permanence, maturity, your mid and later years. This personal history can be a treasure or a curse. It can be deployed by you as an aid to wise decision making or you can choose to just ignore it and blame external life events as the sole cause of any unpleasant situation in your current life. To make constructive use of your Personal History layer rather than letting it make use of you, requires you to be highly conscious of it. For this onion layer can be an aid or a saboteur, depending on whether it is owned and used constructively or denied and left to come back and haunt you when you least expect it.

Present Life

And so you set about designing your future settled life, and how to make it happen. If and when it does, this precious, hard won way of life needs to be actively maintained in order to protect it from being intruded into or sabotaged by any remaining "issues" from your Personal History, Memory Store or Upbringing layers. The insulation and preservation job of this layer – what in the diagram is labelled "Present Life" – is therefore represented in the diagram by a thick dividing line. This layer covers over and separates itself off from old scars or unhealed wounds, just as the real onion generates a thicker layer to protect itself from interior infection or damage. In an emergency, should the outer skin be ruptured, this layer has also to take over its vital protective operations in safely holding in the entire organism, so it has to be tough. The more turbulent your personal history the tougher this protective layer will need to be, for fear of further internal events spoiling your hard won stability – say marriage, children and job satisfaction.

The space between inner and outer skin

On the other hand, someone with a relatively untroubled background may seek something more exciting, risky even, in adult domestic life. They are more open to and interested in their past life, may even wish to continue with it. They may also long for life right outside their "onion", seeing all the chances and choices afforded by the external environment. They have little need of rigid boundaries, feel them as prison walls. Their partner sees in all this nothing but threats to hard won happiness. Much difficulty and even episodes of Depression can arise in the home when two contrasting Personal History layers have wrought very different attitudes and expectations about coupledom, children, money and the rest. Despite long association, the pair may have been unable to come to a compromise about the thickness of that Present Life boundary. Instead of blaming one another for their differences, it might help if both parties inspected one another's personal chronicle to enable them to understand why their partner is so recalcitrant, why one doggedly pursues a sense of security while the other hankers after more adventure, looking fearfully outward toward the barrier posed by the thickest layer of all, the outer onion skin.

The Outer Onion Skin

The outer skin of a real onion is the tough boundary
between the onion's entire interior and the outside,
dangerous as well as nurturing, world. In human terms the
outer skin represents the individual's public "face", the big
chunk of them that other people first meet, oblivious to the
deeper not so "tidied up" chunks inside. In both cases the
"face"/skin has the responsibility for stopping any "untidy"
material that will make them "look bad" from seeping out,
and to prevent any external assault from the environment
from breaking in and damaging vulnerable internal
structures.

Let's take an example. An otherwise contented adult is
destabilised by a brother's death. The brother had been
someone with whom our subject had been in rivalry for
years and whom they hated and loved in equal measure.
The impact of this event from the outer world threatens to
break through the outer skin of the onion, cross the Present
Life and Personal History area and break into the memory
store, reviving all the dormant conflicts safely locked there
till now. Should the subject's tough outside skin and the
next "Present Life" layer beneath it not be robust enough
to act as a buffer between the outside world and the
deeper inner layers, our subject's sense of a coherent Self is
compromised and the chances of an episode of Depression
or other mental health problem is increased.

Outside the onion

Our daily lives are full of pressures from every quarter. We have money worries, career demands, tricky relationships to negotiate, exams to pass, illnesses to battle with, elderly parents to care for, the question of what to get for dinner tonight, finding time to exercise. The list is endless. The pressures of themselves don't cause the Depressions but they can weaken our resistance to it. It's noticeable that some people appear to withstand enormous pressure and others can bear very little. Why?

You need to imagine the usual tumult going on inside the onion (fragile relations with the Self, memories threatening their return, problematic residues of childhood, unstable personal history, unhelpful genes) pushing *outward*, demanding expression and resolution in the external world. Simultaneous real life issues are hammering at that onion from the outside causing reactions from *within*. No wonder we sometimes need to grow a thicker skin!

More external pressure can be borne by the individual with strong onion layers – good current emotional attachments, a reasonably happy childhood, a relatively peaceful and secure memory store and lucky genes. Less fortunate folk appear more vulnerable to an outside observer because they're necessarily working so hard at their inner, unresolved agendas most of the time that there's little energy left over for handling external crises or day to day domestic ones. These remain low on their psychological "to do" list. Yet other people ignore a rumbling inner world (its origins too frightening to contemplate) so long as their present day relationships and social lives compensate for earlier deficits, deprivations and conflicts. Thus their energies are invested outside their onion or in the area between the two thick layers (The Present Life layer and the Outer Skin), in order to keep this state of affairs going. They appear more adept at dealing with the outside world, but who knows what's going on inside that's being so efficiently defended?

The Outer Skin and the second Present Life layer regulate the exchange of all these forces across their boundaries, in whichever direction they flow, trying to maintain sufficient equilibrium to keep the whole human onion intact, in other words mentally healthy. In a real onion the outer skin protects the inner layers from getting bruised and possibly dying, while stopping delicate internal structures that are trying to grow or heal, or infections wanting to spread, from spilling out. All living things and systems share this structure in varying degrees of complexity and we humans are no different.

It's important not to see the concentric circles of the diagram as rigid impermeable walls. They are drawn this way solely for clarity and convenience. The contents of the spaces between the circles (see labels) flow into one another, competing or combining with each other, boosting or diminishing the effect of one another upon the "onion" as a whole. Even if you have a fairly contented life now and it seems unremarkable to you, a closer inspection of your "onion" is almost certain to reveal earlier tensions between the various forces crossing and re-crossing its layers, before that way of life got bedded in. Mira just could not see that all this onion stuff had any relevance for her.

Mira's "boring" story

Some years ago I had a therapist friend who was rather rich and enjoyed the benefit of a live-in nanny whose multi-talented husband was the gardener and odd jobs man. The three of us women often met for coffee at my friend's home. Mira liked to tease us, rolling her eyes and yawning ostentatiously whenever we talked about psychology and therapy. One day she challenged us. "Look here, I'm perfectly ordinary, happily married, got a nice job and lovely flat, no hang ups. All that stuff about childhood things forming you, it's rubbish. Life is just luck, accident. I tell you what, ask me anything, go on, anything. You won't find a single thing that influenced my journey through life. I'm psychologically the most boring but happy person you've ever met. My background is irrelevant to how I turned out."

My friend, her employer and pal, picked up the gauntlet and this is what materialised.

Mira came from a big family, which she chuckled about. They were a superstitious lot, going back at least three generations. To my friend and I these family tales amounted to accounts of obsessive compulsive behaviours and they seemed rife. Aunts, uncles, cousins, all seemed affected though only one ever had a diagnosis and treatment. Learned responses or genes? These behaviours were regarded as dotty and tolerated by all, frequently joked about. Mira too found them amusing, not at all worrying. A typical story was the one about Auntie Iris who was summoned for jury duty and refused to enter the courtroom before she'd polished all the brass door knobs. As he left the court the judge was alleged to have commented approvingly on their shine!

Mira grew up with several brothers and sisters in a warm household, her parents happy together though Dad was always jittery, worrying all the time about his job running his lordship's stables. Eventually he took early retirement and devoted himself to his garden and his own horse. Mira adored him and admitted it upset her whenever he "fussed and bothered over every detail, getting more and more wound up". Nevertheless she felt obliged to go along with the family myth, at least outwardly, that this was just a bit of eccentricity. Like everyone else she tried to jolly him out of it. Her siblings were happy, but "fusspots" as well. Her mother was the only really calm one and she and Mira got on well.

No obsessional thoughts or behaviours (as defined by my friend and I, not Mira) troubled Mira until she reached her teens and school exams. She was bright so was encouraged (pressured?) to try for a prestigious university but she'd never felt herself to be intellectually inclined. Boyfriends and the social world into which she was pitched at the same time all conspired to stress her. Only home and family felt safe. Each time she made forays into the wider adolescent world, tried to compete, as she put it, she felt anxious and miserable and began using ritualistic (she called them "peculiar and daft") behaviours to relieve her tension. Having subliminally learned from years of watching her dad, she must have recognised the link between the pressures of conventional achievement and her "weird" rituals, for she found herself withdrawing from all the expectations placed upon her. She preferred to live quietly, tending and riding the family horse, and baby-sitting for pocket money.

In time she took a childcare course which she loved. She didn't date until she met her husband through her church, and they went to live in a quiet village away from the hurly burly of the market town where she grew up. All her rituals vanished.

"You see, I told you, boring story," Mira triumphantly proclaimed.

My therapist friend would not give up. "OK, so your life has turned out nicely, just the way you wanted it, but have you asked yourself why? Given what you've just told us, think of the different ways your life might have gone. What if your genetic proclivity to "fussing" had been stronger, or your childrearing less loving and supportive? What if your mum hadn't offset the model laid down by your dad? Can't you see that your nice family provided the conditions for you to grow into someone decisive, someone with the confidence to contravene the plan laid down for you by school and your peers? You broke the mould without feeling a failure – how many people can do that? That choice says a lot about your good relationship with your Self. And that in turn is down to your folks and your capacity to make good use of them, not luck!"

Mira pulled a face and my friend, a professional lecturer as well as a therapist, pushed on.

"Think about becoming a teenager, Mira. Without being consciously aware of it at the time, you must have been affected by all those memories of your dad's sufferings, how as a kid you couldn't really help; but you were here for him now and needed things to stay like that. At the same time some part of you recognised your propensity for reacting to stress the same way he did, and what it had cost him. Rather than label yourself a misfit, a failure, as he had, you confidently rejected the ambitious future others expected of you. Also, of course, not leaving for university or getting married early meant you could stay with him till you were ready to go in your own time. Heavens Mira, without that positive start in your family you may have gone along with those external demands on you. You might have got depressed at losing your family long before you were ready, grieved over abandoning your lovely dad. You might have been pushed into a career and failed at it, the stress of it all making you ill with those rituals you seem to find so funny. Your contentment isn't just happenstance: you were *enabled* to shape your own life and you seized the chance."

"Codswallop!" declared Mira, all the same looking a bit shaken. I banged the table and demanded a truce. We all laughed, helping ourselves to another slice of Mira's excellent lemon drizzle cake.

This is a clear case of Nurture winning out over Nature (assuming that the family trait was a genetic predisposition and not behaviours learned via unconscious imitation). Despite a pronounced family history, sound relationships in Mira's home appeared to operate as an antidote. Mira's denial of the seriousness of the family members' symptoms helped her normalise her family's traits so she didn't have to worry about them until she was old enough to shape her own future and deal with them in herself; but the denial was only partial, as her self-preserving decisions about her future confirms.

Whatever you make of your childhood and the key relationships that followed, however valiantly you fought, Nature sometimes wins out anyway. You will have met people who seem mature, fulfilled, get on very well with themselves and others, show all signs of being well-adjusted, even happy. Still the axe of Depressive illness falls, sometimes repeatedly, and apparently unrelated to especial life events. They shouldn't be blamed or blame themselves, nor subject themselves or be subjected to interminable therapy as if there is some elusive mystery to be dug up that will solve everything. This happens all too often however and only makes matters worse. Geneticists, neurobiologists and chemists are all working assiduously to relieve cases like this, but our knowledge remains patchy and inconclusive. Even if there were a mystery to be exhumed, some kinds of personality (Mira's, for example) are fundamentally and resolutely opposed to looking inward and backwards. As the saying goes, they can be taken to the water (of therapy) but they can't be made to drink!

Benevolent, enlightened childrearing doesn't automatically guarantee you a Depression-free life in the future, though the odds may be weighted in your favour. Neither does a background of Depressions in the family, an unhappy childhood, and some awful memories lurking about in your store, necessarily prevent you from enjoying a happy life in the present. Indeed, strong loving attachments to others in the present can go a long way to reducing, neutralising or even countermanding negative past experiences while preventing the burgeoning of genetic leanings into Depression proper.

However, reliance on just one onion layer (say a contented present life) is risky. Should current secure ties be broken, due to divorce, say, or a loved one's death, an extramarital affair or a business failure, then that protective Present Life layer can collapse, leaving the underlying layers exposed. If these are in a sufficiently robust condition they will hold firm and even temporarily take over the function of showing a reasonably okay "face" to the world until that layer can regenerate (till new affirming relationships are made in other words). But if a crammed memory store is now laid open, the delicacy of your relations with your Self uncovered, your questionable personal history laid bare such that all signs now point to a repetition of old mistakes, what chance is there of you staying well, especially if there are no replacement options on the horizon?

An individual's apparent toleration of stress and misfortune is not proof of moral fibre, or even mental health. Neither is the temporary inability to bear it a sign of weakness: you can be strong and resilient on the inside and not on the outside, and vice versa. These are purely psychodynamic (literally "mind movement") matters, as I hope this chapter has shown. All our onions have the same layers but are configured in endless combinations.

Chapter 3

Two Stories, Big 'D' and Little 'd'

In this chapter I will discuss two Depressions: a very serious mid-life one which came apparently out of the blue, and another where an otherwise happy man failed to keep his childhood trauma locked away. In both cases I illustrate the significance of family involvement, both in causation and in healing.

Penny's story

Back in the sixties, barely out of our teens, my best friend Val and I were training as mental nurses (as they were called then) in a massive Victorian hospital on the Eastern edges of London. We were keen students, in our second year now, and we arrogantly assumed that we'd seen it all. Penny was to teach us some humility.

Val had recently met Brian at a jazz club and regaled me endlessly with his wonderful qualities. Soon she was invited to meet his family and afterwards told me every detail.

Brian had a married brother in BBC radio. A first baby was on the way. Dad was in insurance, "a bit of an old woman but a sweetie". Mum, mid-fifties, was "warm and cuddly", taught ballet and tap to children. Her name was Penny and she had been married to Harry for thirty allegedly contented years.

The relationship with Brian progressed smoothly; we were able to talk about other things for a change. Then one day Val reported that Penny was unwell, couldn't even manage her usual slap-up Sunday roast that Val always looked forward to (Val and I were daily subjected to terrible hospital food). Penny's hands had developed an intermittent but distinct tremor, her lower lip wobbled when she spoke, and her feet were unsteady. She "rested" on the settee all day, while Harry brought endless cups of tea she didn't want, puffing and patting her cushions, constantly urging her to take it easy. This of course had the opposite effect, made her more agitated (much to Val's disgust – she bullied him into phoning the GP, amazed he'd been too reluctant to "bother" him before now).

That same day the young doctor arrived after his surgery (yes, they could in those days), gave her a thorough examination and took some blood samples. Val and I mused about diagnosis, clearly something neurological. Could it be Parkinson's, one of the epilepsies, some sort of wasting disease? Later on she was bundled into taxis for X-rays and neurological tests at the local hospital, but nothing was found. The poor doctor was at a loss, muttered about viruses and tropical diseases, talked to his superiors, but got nowhere.

The symptoms got worse and worse, the doctor increasing his visits, clearly frightened and out of control. On her and Brian's weekend visits, Val now spent more time at Penny's bedside, the settee having been abandoned. Dad kept proffering food from which she turned away, though Val managed to get her to sip some fluids. She seemed increasingly vague and tottery, always wanting sleep though she only dozed. There was a bedpan for weekdays, but Penny let Val escort her to the toilet at weekends, leaning heavily on her arm. She would sit on the toilet a-tremble and incoherently muttering for a long time, pale, thin, exhausted yet agitated, before she could summon the strength to return to bed. With "old fusspot" out of the way, Val took the lavatorial opportunity to do what she had never so far dreamt of doing – asking nosy questions.

As Penny's facial muscles fought to get out "b-b-b-" and "c-c-c-" from between her slackened, drooping lips, it struck a rather desperate Val that there might be some clue here. "Penny, are you trying to say something?" Penny sat staring at the frosted toilet window, apparently lost to her own world. The gibberish seemed a conversation – if it was a conversation – with herself rather than any attempt to communicate. Dreading she might do damage (we had had it drilled into us: if you can't do any good for heaven's sake *do no harm*), Val urged: "Penny, look at me, *look* at me". And she did. "B-b-b- baby" she said, perfectly clearly. Val saw on Penny's waxen face what she had never seen before – tears.

Frail and shaking, Penny finally got out her story, a single word at a time. The "c-c-c" turned out to be "k-k-k-kill". She had killed her first baby and wanted to die. She was evil. Nowadays we would refer to it as a cot death, but a sleepless young Penny had taken the crying infant to her bed and in the night it had suffocated. The doctors said she must have rolled over on top of the child and killed it. She was a murderer.

Val was shocked. How could she have missed it all these weeks and months? This was some kind of massive Depression. Bodily, Penny was almost at the point of stupor. If she slowed down any more she would die, her suicidal wishes granted. (Poor Val was in tears of self-reproach when she told me all this.) She phoned the doctor at once.

Penny was admitted to the acute ward of our very own hospital the next day. She was given eight E.C.T.s (electro convulsive therapy) within six weeks, rehydrated, pumped with vitamins and other supplements, and then nothing but rest and more rest for a further week. She returned home right as rain except for some patchy memory loss which didn't seem to trouble her.

The dead baby was not mentioned again and normal life in the household resumed. Val completed her training, before marrying Brian and having a lovely baby a year or so later.

Penny remained well, though according to Val her husband sometimes irritated her, treating her like a Ming vase.

Around five years after the breakdown, now working in different hospitals and rarely able to meet, Val and I finally got together for a proper weekend break. I asked after Penny. Apart from the mother-in-law connection she had become an important figure to us in our professional lives. She it was who'd brought us face to face with what we scoured old text books to find – "involutional melancholia", or midlife Depression as we would say today. She was still well and seemed happy, though was thinking about cutting down on the dance classes and doing a history course at the local college. She enjoyed her grandchildren – Brian's brother now had three to add to Val's two.

The only blip, as Val called it, had been about eighteen months ago when Penny began talking wistfully to Val about the lost baby, but with no accompanying physical symptoms. There was no psychotherapy on the NHS in those days (and precious little now), so, despite her socialist principles, she'd had to "go private", arranged somehow by the young doctor who still felt bad about his earlier psychiatric ignorance. After a few months, she'd told Val how she had come to terms with the death, could accept what happened with sadness and regret but none of the old grief and self-hatred that had emerged during the breakdown.

Discussion

This illness is still debated today in psychiatric circles. Is it a standalone condition, relatively rare, or can it be lumped together with other psychotic (out of touch with reality) Depressive disorders and isn't necessarily related to the mid-life period at all? Does it matter, as the same antidepressant drug groups plus an antipsychotic drug seem to make similar inroads? Psychiatric classifications are always changing and it can be hard to keep up. It's fair to state though that there are many Pennys and her male counterparts out there, people who have never been ill before and may never be ill again, but who for want of proper diagnosis could die. Of course these days they never reach physical stupor, due to eventual recognition and treatment. Diagnosis can be rather late though, as no one expects "normal" folk to undergo such a dramatic illness without any identifiable cause.

The usual picture is of slow onset in a middle-aged person, with bodily symptoms that get gradually worse, and a low mood which they may not even be aware of or are unable to articulate. It's often misunderstood, seen as the effects of ageing, or in women just (!) the menopause. As the Depression progresses, guilt, shame and self-loathing become prominent, though not necessarily verbalised –

indeed speech may become too much of an effort. Some appear to just gradually decay, retire into silence and apathy. In the old days, before the advent of antidepressants, the condition became chronic. Mental hospitals were full of such people, hence the dusty old book we found in the hospital library, with black and white etchings of skinny, head-hanging lost souls curled up on mattresses or sagging like rag dolls in armchairs. These were contemporary illustrations of melancholia. How times had moved on.

But what are we to make of Penny's tragic memories? Were they the cause or the result of her Depression? Would she have become ill anyway, given her genes, about which we know nothing? What about her age, her hormones, her childhood? Once her GP realised what was happening, he quizzed his weary patient and her husband too, about her family and marital history – nothing. Had she suffered any previous episodes? None. She'd been a happy, rather indulged only child with a doting daddy (not unlike Harry). By then she'd stopped muttering about the baby, even to Val, and become increasingly withdrawn. Unwilling to distress her further, he left that topic alone.

Putting aside the awful symptoms of Penny's illness for a moment, focussing on her as a person instead of a patient, how might this Depression have come about? Were there any warning signs? Consider first her marriage to Harry, the "old woman but a sweetie". Clearly devoted to Penny, terrified by her symptoms, he nonetheless downplayed them, tried to render them safe, for himself as much as her: "Just a bit of flu' love, better soon", "You've overdone the classes, not getting any younger you know", "Get yourself some rest. Here's a nice cuppa." How the already semi-comatose Penny was supposed to drink and sleep at the same time incensed Val, whose nursing instincts were to make Penny comfortable and just sit with her quietly. "How has she borne his suffocating protectiveness for thirty years?" Val would demand of me. "He won't let the woman breathe!"

However, during all those years of marriage, who was really looking after whom? Penny had apparently coped well with her baby's death, just went quiet for a while, everyone rallying round until she recovered. Did she ever recover though? Could she have walled up inside herself the devastating guilt and pain she experienced, knowing Harry could never deal with it on top of his own grief? I was astonished to learn from Val that the couple had never ever spoken of the child once the funeral had taken place. Not only that, but both Brian and his older brother had no idea there had ever been a dead baby!

There are several other strands worth examining. In the period just precluding the onset of her breakdown, Penny's oldest son was about to become a father. The imminent arrival of a living infant may have seriously rattled the door of Penny's memory store. And what about her job? Her aching joints in the dance classes must have confronted her with middle age and an increasingly heavy and round figure. Progesterone was falling rapidly and perhaps she questioned her sexual desirability. As ever, she'd have kept her private preoccupations from Harry. Though eagerly awaiting retirement and his vegetable plot, it seemed unlikely he would have been able to reassure her much anyway. The arrival of Val on the scene must have reminded her too that, while the younger woman's career was just beginning, her own was in decline. Her role as Mother was no consolation either as her two sons had now flown the nest. Her life was closing down with very little opening up. Put all this together. The stage was clearly set for a possible little 'd' at least. Could it have been some combination of all these factors that turned low mood into near tragedy? Would she still have become so ill had there not been so many elements operating together? I don't know, but an alert observer who knew Penny well might have seen her big 'D' coming much earlier and taken appropriate action.

Eugene and Antony's story

In contrast to Penny's life-threatening illness, let's now look at two linked, but less clear-cut, cases of little 'd'.

Eugene was my new therapy client, an eminent barrister, impeccably suited, polished shoes you could see your face in, manicured fingernails. He explained in our first session

that he'd come to "tie up some loose ends". He was having
what he called day pictures: "I believe you people call them
flashbacks?" It seems the pictures had lately woken him
at night as well, and once visited him whilst on his feet
in court, which understandably panicked him into seeing
someone. "But before I continue," he said crisply, "you have
to realise that on no account do I wish to have you poking
about in my current life. You should know I am happily
married. I have a son approaching A-levels who is totally
normal and well-adjusted. I am, if I say so myself, very
successful in my work. I get on well with my colleagues in
chambers. I eat properly and exercise regularly. You are to
leave all that alone. Are we clear?"

He was much less self-assured as he told me about the
loose ends. His rich father had been a minor politician but
an ambitious one. His money, his family and his public
school background gave him access to the highest echelons
of society. It seems his ambition got the better of him
however, for he was exposed across every newspaper in
the land, along with his cronies, for implicating himself in
something that these days would approximate to election
rigging. Forgery, blackmail, vast sums of laundered money
were involved. Eugene was twelve at the time, and taken
briskly out of his new school when the scandal broke. All he
understood was that some terrible shame had befallen his
family, who went into hiding in the wilds of Scotland, while
his father languished in prison. His mother refused to visit,
sued for divorce, after which his father hanged himself in

his cell. It was this picture of his father swinging "with no one to cut him down" that was haunting Eugene.

After only a few sessions he announced he was ready to go. I had done very little but the pictures had gone. "I presume there's some sort of curative magic in talking out loud about it," he said, "you know, with a witness present," and off he went. Six weeks later he phoned to make an appointment for his son. "I'm afraid he seems to be depressed," he confided, with a bit of a tut-tut in his voice. I said that, before we rushed into anything, perhaps he might come himself, talk it over with me so I could properly understand. I felt there was much unfinished business here.

Antony, his son, had been studying hard for his exams, handing over his Smartphone to his mother so he wouldn't be tempted. He didn't take drugs, or bring home unsuitable girl- or boyfriends, went to bed at ten, refused junk food and never touched alcohol. His few friends were "decent lads from good homes". He'd never given Eugene any problems till now. He'd started hibernating in his room, taking his food there, sleeping there the second he got back from school, then staying up till all hours "just mooching about, those bloody earphones". He never watched the TV with his mum any more, or larked about with her like he used to when Eugene was late home from chambers or in his study. She missed him. He wasn't showering or even combing his hair, now it was school holidays. He wore the same clothes for days on end. Usually good mannered, he hardly spoke. When asked what was wrong, he just grunted that he was okay and left the room.

"Lilian and I are worried sick. What else can we do? We've sat him down and talked to him, though Lilian's better at this sort of thing. Is it girl trouble? Is someone threatening him, social media bullying or something. Is he gay? Lonely? Worried about his body image? Is he stressed? What about a big holiday after exams, a cruise maybe? No response, just slouches off to his bedroom. Then we tried to get him to "man up" as they say, to think of his future prospects, pull himself together. Could he not see how lucky he was compared to some of the kids you see on television, hoodies carrying knives and whatnot. Had he spared a thought for us, the things we'd given him, his private school, our lovely house, the best trainers, the latest phones. . ."

"Had you thought of leaving him alone?"

"*What. . . . . . . ?*"

This led to a discussion about teenage emotional development, the normal need to brood, ask questions about identity, relationships, the meaning of the universe; the natural urge to quietly or loudly rebel, become your own person, not what had always been demanded of you. Could Antony have been robbed of his healthy teenage angst, forced to accept all his heart desired till he realised he desired something different? Had his parents nearly killed him with kindness in this regard, and now he was fighting back? I looked at Eugene's face. I could have been talking Martian. We had to slow down.

I was amazed by this intelligent, well-read man's naivety when it came to psychology. (It paralleled my own ignorance of the law.) Naturally we should keep an eye on the lad, I proffered, but at last he was breaking the goody two-shoes mould and perhaps that was all for the best in the end. "You sound like Lilian," he grumbled.

My surmise at that time was that young Antony was probably healthily miserable, struggling to grow up and away from his loving but over monitoring parents, especially Eugene. Apparently Lilian was sad, but accepting that a son could not be at her apron strings forever.

Eugene was somewhat indignant at my suggestion that his own "depression" never mind Antony's, might be the more important issue here. Moreover, if the mood problem he so hotly contested was not granted due respect and attention, it could one day turn into the serious more chronic kind. He confessed somewhat grudgingly that he'd been taking naps and rather more brandy than usual in his study lately, and that Lilian had complained of his irritability to both her and Antony. He adored his son, so was feeling horribly guilty about his current angry feelings towards him. "I don't want to hate the boy, it's not right, but he's – well – letting the side down."

Further work with Eugene uncovered the true reasons behind this blaming of his son. We saw how his own painful childhood had been relegated to a lead canister and dropped in the sea. He refused to ever think about it, had felt physically sick at having to tell me about his father's suicide. He'd covered over those terrible memories with a distinguished career, a happy marriage, a perfect home, a *perfect child*. Under no circumstances must this hard won position be challenged, as he'd made so plain to me at our first meeting, lest all that misery return. Seeing Antony so gloomy and withdrawn must also have reminded him of himself so many years ago, unable to help his father in prison ("no one to cut him down"), watching his mother's increasing bitterness and drug dependency, feeling friendless in the cold and lonely Scottish highlands. He couldn't help himself way back then, but Antony must not, will not, be allowed to suffer so. Yet the wretched boy just would not do his bit.

We explored Eugene's own personality, in which he was finally taking an interest. His teens had been so tumultuous that no one had had the time to show any concern for his feelings other than to provide the material and bodily necessities; so he hadn't bothered either. He was intrigued now to find he actually possessed an interior world and began to cautiously look round it. Whether genes, early upbringing or another cover-up of the emotional injuries he sustained accounted for it, he recognised his adult Self as the problem solver, the logician, the manager, decision maker, the all-responsible *paterfamilias*. That he himself might have vulnerabilities and needs, low and high moods, had never occurred to him. His sole priority had been to build and sustain an unassailable fortress against the past, an idealised family that would blot out the first one. There was to be no guilt, loneliness or shame this time. Antony was wrecking the plan. The cost of maintaining this unrealisable fantasy was an ongoing little 'd' (that could one day become the big one), of which he'd been totally unaware.

I'm pleased to report that during a long therapy Eugene and I hauled that old canister out of the sea. Eugene gave full compassionate attention to the neglected, bewildered little chap inside him, enabling him to see his own son differently. He stopped designing and polishing Antony and began trying to understand his own Self instead. I am happy to say their relations slowly improved and neither of them fell prey to the big 'D'.

Discussion

This true but disguised story has some instructive aspects. It demonstrates how unresolved or unacknowledged Depression (Eugene's suicidal father, his drug-dependent mother, his own childish despair) does not end with the death of, or denial by, the sufferers, but is passed down in the family culture, to be picked up by the next generations(s). I hope in this case Antony will not have to hand on the family tradition. It shows too, that many people affected by Depression, like Eugene, don't even see their own suffering. This may seem like a blessing, but others usually bear the brunt of it, as did Antony and his mother. It also highlights how some try to control their way out of Depression, by using their authority, intelligence or personality attributes to make others conform to their requirements so as to bring about a spurious peace (Eugene's fanatical pursuit and maintenance of a substitute family that would correct the past). This story of father and son also shows how some descents into major and/or chronic Depression can be forestalled.

Many troubled individuals so fear the search for *meaning* in their symptoms that they resort to emergency *action* instead. In this case it meant Eugene burying unendurable pain, and when it wouldn't stay buried, relocating (dumping?) the ensuing Depression in Antony, before recruiting an expert whose job was to perform a quick fix on the lad without disturbing the *status quo*. Fortunately for us all, I declined that invitation

Chapter 4

Types of Depression – The Mainly Psychiatric Perspective

Nowadays, thanks to search engines, media documentaries and self-help publications, the general public must be quite familiar with these classifications, so this will be but a summary, illustrated with some true but disguised vignettes.

Most diagnoses are based on the degree of Depression – mild to severe – and whether it's associated with some known hormonal, neurological or physical malaise, or painful life event. How long does it last and is it recurrent? Are there delusions and hallucinations? Are there abnormal highs as well as lows? Does the low mood dominate, cover up, override, blend with or even cause other disorders? Once made, these diagnostic labels aren't sacrosanct or necessarily permanent. Over time, signs and symptoms can shift and re-settle, get worse or better, appear and disappear, making it difficult to say precisely where they belong in the psychiatric canon at any one time. Depression is always a mood on the move, even when it's very slow or temporarily stuck. Mercifully it doesn't last forever and even the chronic types enjoy remissions and milder attacks interspersed with the major ones.

Dysthymia and Reactive Depression

Dysthymia is equivalent to this book's little to middling 'd' – qualitatively different to common unhappiness, but still less than big 'D'. The sufferer can function, though far from their best, and misery may persist for a long time, years even, if not taken seriously. Depression is a de-motivator so the afflicted person may never do anything about it. The absence of optimism and an inability to enjoy much are the key indicators. The mood appears to be less pervasive but drags on longer than in acute unipolar Depression (see later). Someone like this is often described as "a depressive personality" and is ignored ("they're always like that, don't take any notice") but they can become more severely depressed at times, necessitating urgent attention. The suicidal risk at those times is very real.

So-called *reactive depression* looks similar but is relatively short lived and appears to be precipitated by some sad or shocking life event. It can occur in anyone, whatever their usual temperament, and is very often related to relationship crises. However, the degree of the person's reaction is beyond what one might expect in the circumstances and does not seem to be improving within the time one might reasonably predict.

Postnatal Depression

Postnatal Depression describes far more than the understandable fatigue and hormonal blues that many mums experience, and can deteriorate (that does not mean it must!) to a state of suicidal despair, accompanied by guilty but murderous wishes toward the infant. Along with other *Psychotic Depressions* there are by that stage delusions (false beliefs that cannot be corrected by rational argument or contrary proofs) and hallucinations (seeing and hearing things that are not there). The new mother is convinced she is evil, not ill, and often thinks she is being judged or persecuted by outside forces. Medical intervention and constant observation is crucial during this phase of the illness. Mercifully some recover before psychosis sets in, but that recovery can be very slow, its effects felt for months and even years if not treated.

Physical Illnesses

Physical illnesses can precipitate little to big 'D' Depression. Imagine living with chronic pain, degenerative disease, immobility, or hormonal disorders (be these permanent or temporary). All are linked with varying degrees of mood imbalance. Consider menstruation and menopause in women or the consequences of testosterone depletion in men. How testing must it be for an elderly couple living day to day with Parkinson's and its attendant mood changes? Or, God forbid, a brain tumour? Imagine in some detail what life is like with type 1 diabetes, contending daily with pumps, injections, pills and/or patches. You have to watch every mouthful because your weight and sugar level is critical; you depend on prescriptions and appointments, regular self-inspection for circulatory problems. You have to explain to people all the time what not to feed you, what they should do if you suddenly collapse (unlikely these days, but still possible). You are never off duty. The stress of such an existence, especially when the newly diagnosed individual is still adjusting to it, can easily tip into loss of hope, especially when other life crises also hit. It isn't sufficient to treat the pancreas or any other organ in isolation from its owner!

In addition to all this stress and suffering another dimension needs considering. Physical illnesses can also be mistaken for Depressions, and vice versa. When thyroid secretion goes haywire, the ensuing symptoms can closely mimic little 'd' or big 'D'. Failure to spot and treat the hormone deficiency causes untold misery, as would a failure to realise that when the thyroid gland is returned to normal but the patient is still very down, the doctor may have two quite unrelated ailments on their hands. Depression combines with other conditions quite often and it's important not to jump to the conclusion that, just because a medical diagnosis has been identified, its corrective treatment will also cure the Depression. It's similarly naïve to say that if it looks like a Depression, it is a Depression so there's no need to search elsewhere. A full medical assessment is important, but should never exclude exploration of the person's psychological life and the quality of their personal relationships, now and in the past. This rounded approach is what we mean by holistic, and will be discussed in the next chapter. Collecting all this data is a very special art however, and central to it is the quality of the relationship between the patient and the person treating them. So here's a cautionary tale for GPs.

A healthy, busy, professional friend of mine in her seventies visited her surgery to ask for a routine prescription for sore eyes. Previously, she and her then doctor had agreed she was to request the drops again should the symptoms return. Her appointment this time was with a new, very young doctor, who examined her, went carefully over her eyes' history, then explained the medical condition in some detail. Thinking her doctor was just doing her job, my friend bore all this patiently until the doctor turned from the computer to face her. "And how do you fill your time, Mrs. Bloggs?"

Shocked, embarrassed and angry, my friend was (unusually) lost for words. She hastened home very upset. She later realised that the GP had been methodically working her way through on-screen tick-boxes that would ensure she'd covered everything properly. But in so doing, my friend had felt she'd been dealt with as an object not a person. She was in her seventies: therefore she must be retired, past it, superfluous to society, hanging about with nothing to do and probably in need of a pottery class or maybe geriatric antidepressants. Well, she had plenty to fill her time with, thank you very much, and was not to be treated in so stereotypical a manner. She would write a letter!

The consultation may well have touched on my friend's latent memories of being lumped together with other "undesirables" in the past — patronised, valueless, just a typical something-or-other, so lip-service and box-ticking will do. She wasn't going to stand for it again. Oversensitive maybe, but her reaction goes to show how easy it is for professional helpers to mean well yet get it so wrong.

Continuing with the physical category, we arrive at the whole area of terminal illness, old age, and the dementias. The absence or unlikelihood of cures in these areas, despite the best palliative care and ongoing research, poses a massive challenge to both the psychiatrist and their patient. There can be no pretence that things are going to get better any time soon. Hope in the form of physical improvement really has gone — this is no Depressive delusion. What routes to other kinds of hope might be open? Pills alone will rarely, if ever, suffice. However sophisticated the medical and chemical regime, the search for meaning, peace and hope in our dotage is our last developmental task on this earth. Wise counsel and trusted company is required for that journey. It may not be a question of *either* pills *or* psychological support, but a matter of *both* medication *and* psychological help in the right combination at the right time. Oh, and what does the ill or elderly person actually *want?* Has anybody asked them?

Bipolar, unipolar and cyclothymia

These are characterised by mood swings, manifested in an extreme and alarming manner in untreated *bipolar*, the ill person alternating between exaltation and despair, being out of touch with reality in both states. *Cyclothymia* is a much toned down version of this. Mild cases can be described as a personality type rather than an illness – the dividing line is fine. The swing in *unipolar* is only one way, seriously down then back to normal, then down again, but for diagnostic purposes it has to be cyclical, not a one-off. Later in this chapter I'll discuss the example of a very public figure whose unipolar is already in the public domain.

Regarding bipolar, some people endure one cycle and rarely, if ever, again; whereas others will have repeated bouts over many years, though early recognition and treatment, with or without maintenance doses of antipsychotic medications, can greatly reduce the impact of the illness on day to day life. You may be sharing an office with someone who is bipolar, the illness either controlled or in remission, and you will never know.

It should also be mentioned that the old term for this disorder was *"manic depression"* and has been recognised for centuries. Some claim that the new term of bipolar is too frequently appended to lesser symptoms, hence the apparent increase in the incidence of the disorder. Others believe that the increase is real and down to the nature of our culture, so dependent on instant gratification and a pill for every time we are frustrated or disappointed. If we have attained happiness and approval from the world, we are worthwhile people; if we are unhappy we must be ill and need help.

There are also people who suffer from a simultaneous mixture of "low" and "high" symptoms. They experience all the energy and restlessness of mania (as it used to be called) without the euphoria, and all the self-chastisement and guilt of the Depression at the same time. The two poles clash, producing unbearable anguish. Clearly these extremely disturbing behaviours need medical management, but in remission sophisticated therapeutic intervention can help the individual find meaning in the illness and especially its likely triggers, given the state of their particular "onion" as described in chapter 2.

You hear many folk declaring (often boasting or joking) that they're bipolar when what they mean is that they easily swing from an up mood to a down one. This is merely a description of temperament. Such trivialising of the actual condition must be galling to genuine sufferers. Bipolar is identified early these days and specific drugs to flatten out the volatility of mood are very effective. Most people have no idea what untreated bipolar, especially in the manic phase, actually looks like, what those who have it so dread happening to them again. Let me take you back to the sixties once more, to my nursing days with Val. We will show you.

Greta's cycle

We were doing our three months' stint on "Disturbed", the last remaining locked ward after recent legislation and the arrival of new medications had made a general throwing away of keys possible. (The drugs were still crude. Many staff complained the old canvas straitjackets had just been exchanged for chemical ones.)

Sister took a phone call, then advised us of an imminent emergency admission. We knew the drill. We prepared the windowless side room, stripped it of anything sharp down to the last splinter, anything that could be swallowed, used as a weapon on self or other, even down to a pencil or comb. No smash-able light bulbs allowed, no uncovered electrical sockets. Satisfied, I pocketed the room's keys. In frilly caps and starched aprons all us nurses then lined up like soldiers along both sides of the corridor behind the locked entrance, ready for anything. It was a matter of pride not to summon nurses from the male side, but they'd been apprised, just in case. The cocktail trolley as we called it, laden with drug-filled syringes, sat ready and waiting in Sister's office.

We heard the wah-wah of the ambulance approaching, took in some deep breaths. As usual one of us – it turned out to be me – was then deputed to go outside and greet the paramedics and the patient. A burly chap reached for the door handles and said to me "stand back, love".

Greta, barefooted, hospital nightgown flying, literally leapt from the ambulance that had strategically parked flush with the now gaping ward door. Her eyes were wild – I could almost see sparks. Her thick frizzy blonde hair stuck out from her head, a crazy nest of knots; her skin glowed with what looked like preternatural health, but two arcs of froth dribbled down either side of her grinning mouth. There was no aggression, no fear, only excitement, an ecstatic joy as she greedily devoured her surroundings. She charged round the ward, dislodging pictures from the wall, upturning chairs like a naughty, giggly child. She banged on every surface as if making music, while dancing and prancing, knees high and head flung back. I could not help but recall the Greek myths I had read at school, the maenads (literally the raving ones) who intoxicated themselves before dancing away days and nights in Dionysian rituals, some dying of exhaustion along the way.

The other end of the ward led onto a tiny concreted courtyard, gate-locked and secluded by high walls of Victorian soot-blackened stone. Other than calling on the men to come and overpower her, all we could do was open the door to it so she could continue her frenzy without harming anyone. None of us nurses could catch her to sedate her. It was like a game of tag to her, all good fun. She shoved us off her, laughing in delight at her own strength (a swimming coach, she was strong as a horse). We followed her every step, making hopeful grabs at her, but she shrieked with laughter and slipped from our grasp each time. Against our will and better judgement we found ourselves infected by her mania. The chase did indeed become a bizarre kind of fun, and to our shame we found ourselves laughing with her and each other.

Eventually she surged back through the door into the ward, three tired nurses trailing behind. She was now covered in dust from the yard, her knees crusty and bleeding. Oblivious to any pain, she knelt by Sister's door and banged on it, laughing: "Open up! Oyez oyez! Open up!" The door did just that, revealing Sister poised with a syringe full to the hilt of Largactil. She nodded meaningfully at us: "Enough. We have to do this." By now Greta was on all fours, bare bottom exposed between the split in her NHS nightie. She was talking to imaginary earwigs on the floor, trying to pull them up through the cracks in the linoleum. Her head was at Sister's feet.

I shot Val a conspiratorial look, saw it was received. "Horsey!" I yelled at Greta, bending down and grinning into her face as if joining her play: "Horsey, horsey!" She remained on all fours and started to buck. I jumped astride her back, a tight grip, and pretended I was a cowboy in the old west. "Giddey up thare, old gal," I hooted. "Them thare steers sure aint gonna move without us!" "Ride a cockhorse to Banbury Cross," she retorted delightedly, about to gallop off with me. But Val and the other nurse seized their chance, dived for her ankles and held on tight. We had her pinned down for a few precious seconds and in went the needle, upper outer quadrant, right buttock. She seemed not to feel a thing. Somewhat half-heartedly I continued playing at cowboys, till she staggered and fell.

Sister locked away the trolley and instructed us that she was not to be disturbed except for an emergency. She took Greta's ashen husband, who had accompanied his wife in the ambulance and witnessed all this, into her office. The poor man was in shock. I suspect medicinal brandy changed hands.

After a week of four hourly sedation in the daytime and barbiturates sufficient to knock out an elephant at night, Greta quietened down and the drugs were slowly withdrawn. Despite the severity of the illness the psychiatrist dare not prescribe ECT, for fear of adverse swings in mood; the treatment in those days could be unpredictable. Dopey and barely able to walk during drug withdrawal, we waited for her to return to normal, in the meantime discreetly attending to her personal hygiene. Then she became almost totally silent, refusing food, unwilling to come out of her side room onto the ward, unwilling to exercise in the courtyard, uninterested in TV, not wishing to chat with us nurses. She wore nothing but penitential grey and black, pleaded to be left alone, but we dared not leave her.

As the last of the drugs drained from her system, she grew agitated, self-hating, ashamed, recalling over and over every detail of her mad behaviour. She begged our forgiveness, demanded we lock her in her room, punish her, give her an overdose of pills. She pleaded with her long-suffering husband to divorce her, find someone else better than her. If we nurses tried to comfort her she would send us away to go and help someone else, someone more deserving than her. After the agitation came a physical and mental torpor, a silent withdrawal and avoidance of human contact that lasted weeks.

We saw Greta through an entire bipolar cycle, from which she did in the end fully recover. We learned that this cycle had repeated itself roughly every five years since she was nineteen. We feared she may one day find herself unable to face another attack.

Unipolar Depression: A TV film

A myth persists that only introverts fall prey to Depression and bright and breezy types don't. Not true. Alistair Campbell made a film for BBC2 in 2019 about his own intermittent Depression and his search for a cure. His public profile is that of a hectically busy modern man, socially, politically and philanthropically active, outgoing and very successful indeed. Yet he tells us that he will know what the day has in store for him mood-wise by whether he has bothered to open the blind on his landing first thing in the morning. It's as if the Depression steals up on him in the night, an alien visitor, and it's some external piece of data – the blind – that informs him whether the visitor is still in residence.

This contrasts with others' experience of recurring Depression, where the person is all too aware of its onset, fights long and hard against it until in the end they accept they're powerless to resist. Perhaps these are the introverts, whereas the extravert is suddenly ambushed by Depression. Perhaps the introvert "chews the cud" slowly, increasingly self-critical, hope fading gradually, till that rumination climaxes into fully fledged Depression; whereas the other lives such a frantic life that all rumination is staved off and staved off – no time, no time! – till the Depression dramatically strikes, seemingly from nowhere.

Despite a loved brother's schizophrenia, alcohol problems and a severe breakdown as a younger adult, Mr. Campbell says in his film that he's unaware of any trauma or significant conflict in his childhood, and on that basis he has decided against psychotherapy. He prefers a rigorous exercise schedule, loyal support from his wife and family, pills that through trial and error he has found most useful, and stress-relieving bagpipe playing. He still suffers, but less than he once did. He seems to have integrated Depression into his life, rather than futilely attempting to banish it or making an enemy of it. Regrettably, unipolar Depression tends to be chronic and is best managed and come to terms with, rather than waging an angry self-defeating war against it, or allowing yourself to feel inferior or a victim because you're cursed with it.

However you experienced your childhood or whether you want to talk about it, counselling and psychotherapy can still be productive in learning how to co-exist with the disorder without it dominating your total outlook. When that unstoppable rumination takes over, you may as well take advantage of those unavoidable awful thoughts. Shared, they sometimes throw much light on past matters less resolved than you thought. Letting them emerge in their own time (not having them dragged out of you!) can be immensely relieving. Even if childhood and later difficult relationships are not discussed, how to more creatively handle the present is always worth a good old chinwag with someone who has seen an awful lot of unipolar.

Also, of course, people with unipolar have other, unrelated issues they may want help with, like Jo (see below) whose cyclothymia didn't seem to bother him at all; he wanted help with his marriage. Unipolar alone (or any other type of Depression) doesn't have to define who you are. Having said that, it has to be admitted that those horrible downward swings may quite seriously impinge upon a person's central relationships at times, and so they may be brought into counselling as a significant but secondary matter.

Jo's cyclothymia

Jo was a BT engineer who came to see me claiming he'd never had a day's illness, mental or physical, in his life. He was chatty and charming and loved to regale me with the latest jokes doing the rounds at work. But some weeks he would fall quiet and inward looking, scarcely able to raise a smile. There was a lot of weariness and sighing if I prodded him for a response.

He was in his early forties and had been married for fourteen years to "Lovely Louise". All the same, he had for the past two years carried on a clandestine affair with an unmarried work colleague, who was lately pressing him to leave his wife. He admitted ruefully that he wanted them both, but now risked losing the pair of them, as his wife had found about the other woman on discovering restaurant receipts in his van's glove box. He had to make a decision. "You counselling folk don't just do fruit loops, do you? You help with relationships and that?"

As our work advanced, he grew more thoughtful about his past, what these two women might represent for him in terms of his upbringing in a children's home, then foster care. Eventually he chose to "take a bit of a break" from both women and rented a flat by himself. To his surprise he found he rather liked the new arrangement; it gave him time to think rather than rushing at things. Both women had given him six months to make up his mind. I noticed that, despite finding a temporary sense of stability, his moods continued to go up and down in a swift but orderly sequence, irrespective of what was happening in his life. When I commented on this he grinned and explained. In his up phase he loved to tell a tale and I watched with interest as his excitement accelerated.

"I'm a bit of a cosmologist you know – moon landings, space travel, is there life on Mars, all that. They call me Moody Rudi at work – Russians, space race and everything. Proper nerd I was as a kid, read all the books about it, the history, watched the TV documentaries. But even then I noticed the moods, couldn't understand 'em at all. One week chipper, the next it was like the dark side of the moon in my head. Just shoved it all to one side in the end, carried on regardless, like I did with this women thing before you made me dig it all up."

He paused for effect. "Then one day I *saw* myself, right there in the sky. It all made sense, the moods, the whole thing. I felt so much better after that – ha-ha, no shrinks required. What happened was, our teacher dished out goggles and took us to see a partial eclipse, my first. . ."

He described how the other kids sang in the bus, boisterous, relishing the freedom from lessons; how they piled out onto the grass, tucked into their sandwiches and coke, ignoring their teacher who kept checking his watch. Soon they were called to order, gathered round, took out their goggles and restlessly waited, jostling each other. Jo was the only reverent one, already gazing at the heavens.

At the appointed time the sky began to darken into a metallic grey, with an eerie glare that made the watchers screw up their eyes. Then all the birds stopped twittering. No leaf stirred, no animal or insect moved, not a blade of grass quivered. The earth held absolutely still. The scared children fell silent. As the mighty shadow began its slow, inexorable journey across the lower half of the sun, Jo had his epiphany. The solar system was doing its thing, no one and nothing could stop it. Mere humans could only sit it out, watch and wait. *His moods were just the same!* First came the warning silence, then the shadow. After that, a slice of his mind was utterly black, dead, till his eclipse had passed and the sun reclaimed its radiance till the next time. "Always the same, the certainty comforting. You could foresee it all, you knew exactly what was coming and what was going."

Jo had been mesmerised by a celestial process that precisely reflected what regularly happened in his brain. This reassured him that his mood cycle was congruent with, in harmony with, the eternal laws of the universe. He was actually *all right*. It was as if his moods were ordained, natural. Since then he'd probably assumed that other people went through cycles just like his, and if they didn't there must be something wrong with them. Overall he was on good terms with his Self, which was why he hadn't thought to mention the mood swings in the therapy.

It's this clear identification of a point of no return, this sense of inevitability, the impotence in the face of something bigger than oneself, that distinguishes cyclothymia from ordinary low mood, as well as the absolute faith in the sun's return. In psychotic Depression the eclipse is total. In mania the sun explodes.

I expected Jo's moods to somehow synchronise with his love life. Perhaps one of his women suited him better when he was up, the other when he was down. I toyed with all sorts of possibilities. In the end I had to accept there was no correlation whatever between his cyclothymia and his relationships; they operated quite independently of each other. We counsellors and therapists are always looking for links and patterns in our clients' psychology, but this case warns us against making convenient and tidy formulations without evidence.

Discussion

I'm so glad that the professions of medicine, counselling, psychiatry and psychology are growing ever more co-operative and mutually sympathetic, given their shared mission to understand and alleviate psychic distress. The mingling of and arguing over their theories, practices and terminologies must be confusing to many, but at least it shows we are finally leaving behind that sad era when different helping professions competed for legitimacy in the public eye, and bitterly defended their clinical territory in academic and scientific circles. As the provision of medical, social and mental health services grows more unified, all the professionals will hopefully come together to forge a more coherent and integrated way of mapping the largely undiscovered country constituted by the Depressions. One day we might all speak the same language.

Before we leave this "mainly psychiatric" chapter, we should perhaps remind ourselves of any prejudice we might harbour against or in favour of that particular profession. Psychiatrists are not Svengalis, able to infiltrate and control the most private recesses of our minds. Neither can they perform the healing miracles which so many long for: their treatment tools are limited. And just because mental illness is the psychiatrist's special domain, it doesn't mean they pathologise everybody, have scant regard for ordinary human unhappiness or relationship problems. They are not soulless materialists seeing only chemistry and neurons where a real person ought to be.

Finally, a word on self-help manuals. They can be very useful, but some erroneously imply that illness doesn't really exist in this field, all "depression" being "normal". The motive may be to cheer up the unhappy reader (why else would they be reading about the Depressions?), but concealing or downplaying the truth is as unhelpful as it is unethical. The Depressions cover a very wide spectrum, and sufferers in my view are entitled to work out, through accessing internal (that onion again) and external information, just which section of the range they're trying to come to terms with at any one moment.

Chapter 5

Types of Depression – The Psychological Perspective

The Depressions don't exist in isolation from their setting. What and who is affecting and being affected by this pervasive mood change? What led up to it and what's maintaining it or enabling it to get better? In other words how does the person's background – family, job, friends, partners, or lack of these-– influence their grim condition and their attitude towards it? A huge part of that background, of course, is the relationship they have shaped over time to their own Self, the internal setting so to speak. How they think and feel about their Self when not in the grip of Depression tells much about whether, when and under what conditions they might again succumb. All this constitutes the psychological/interpersonal rather than the psychiatric perspective (it's also referred to as the holistic approach). Often both perspectives are essential for recovery.

In a later chapter we'll consider ways that any helper, be they friend, relative or counsellor, can support someone who has lost control of their mood in this way, how best to accompany them through the process and out the other side. For no matter how much a sufferer longs to be well, they can't loosen Depression's vice-like grip by simply making a brave decision: the will is paralysed and for a time "cure" is not an option. Unhappiness can be tolerated for there's a rationale to explain it and an end is in sight; but in Depression the inability to penetrate the consuming dark renders the sufferer impotent: some will kill themselves rather than endure that loss of autonomy. Friends and partners willing to stick with the person through the course of their Depression until they are restored to wellbeing truly are worth their weight in gold. Living with someone this low isn't easy.

For now though, we'll focus on the Depressions as syndromes, groups of co-existing human determinants, not single entities, "diseases" that whiz through the air to inexplicably drop on your lap (though it's described that way by some). The sufferer's *subjective experience and interpretation of* their present and past relationships (personal, familial, professional), as well as what is *objectively* happening in those relationships right now, all help or aggravate their prevailing mood state. It has to be remembered, too, that the people they interact with also interpret and attribute meaning to what's going on between themselves and our sufferer; so it's a moot point as to what belongs to whom, whose perceived reality is the right one. Many Depression-prone people can't accurately distinguish between their own judgement and others', and end up taking on self-condemnatory views that don't properly belong to them. They are expert at absorbing blame and criticism: they have but a flimsy filter between their own value system and others', no confidence in their own point of view. They are all too ready to have their most damning fears about themselves confirmed. If they are like this when well, it's but a short step to Depression when things go wrong.

This may be a good juncture to remind the reader about my terminology. Big 'D' in this text refers not only to the major and mostly psychotic Depressions in particular, but is also used as an umbrella term whenever we are talking about all the types collectively. Little 'd' is used, rather than just "depression", to emphasise the difference between a temporary *disorder* of mood rather than an unhappy response to unfortunate circumstances. Little 'd' separates the state under discussion from its vernacular usage.

To demonstrate the powerful influence of the psychological and interpersonal context on the person's ailing mood, I will share some examples of Depressions that occur at nodal points in the human life cycle. Arrival at that point does not of itself bring about persistent low mood – indeed it can be cause for rejoicing and celebratory ritual, such as an eighteenth birthday party, a wedding or collecting a degree. Not everyone hits a midlife crisis the day they hit forty or fifty. Not all retirees fall into inertia and obscurity.

But these periods of change so often act as a catalyst, bring to the fore issues the person may have had lying about for ages at the back of their minds, but put off for a later date. This time has now come.

As each phase of life segues into another – school to work perhaps, newly-wed to mother, husband to widow, boss to retiree – a process of letting go, of *separation* occurs. Giving up what has been routine, familiar, affirming, then moving into unknown territory, however exciting, can feel threatening. It will be secure and reliable personal relationships mixed with belief in the Self that can bridge the gap. Yet the new demands of the coming phase of life can de-stabilise those very attachments to Self and others so needed at this precarious time. Thus we see how progress and separation, gain and loss go hand in hand in the normal human life cycle.

Some folk weather a new developmental phase, some celebrate it, some become Depressed. What accounts for the difference? Let's try to answer this by way of examples that focus on the main elements alluded to so far – *current relationships, personal history, separation* and *attitude to Self* that cluster so prominently in many Depressions. Restricting our attention to simple signs and symptoms is reductive cause-and-effect thinking that's insulting to sufferers and doesn't help us to fully comprehend the complex nature of the Depressions.

Developmental phases

Birth (for both parties)

Being born must be pretty traumatic for a baby. Having
floated blissfully in warm amniotic fluid, cushioned by a
nutritional placenta, carried everywhere by a host body that
provided everything you needed, you're suddenly thrust
willy-nilly into a loud, bright, cold world where your body
is bare of any surrounding comforts, any warmth, any
soothing sounds of a heartbeat. Yet infants on the whole
survive. What does that first experience lay down in the
still-forming brain pathways that for the rest of its life
will inform the organism how to react to shock, newness?
Some babies engage with the world howling in protest;
others lay back, turn away defeated, have to be slapped into
using their lungs. What dictates which infant reacts with a
scream and which not even a whimper? Is the tendency to
Depression already evident?

Does a comforting relationship with the breast or bottle
compensate for being hurled into the world in so rude a
fashion? Do mother's arms console the infant for the loss
of their former safe universe? Can the birth terror be laid
to rest? Mother too, has been subjected to this massive,
uncontrollable upheaval in her mind/body, her total
organism on the rack. She is expected to cope, for she's
grown up and in charge. Or is she? If she doesn't feel in
charge, imagine her guilt, her self-hatred, her shame.

Kathleen's story (wife to mother)

Kathleen was pregnant for the second time. She came into therapy because she feared another postnatal breakdown. In her early thirties, she worked in an NHS laboratory as a microbiologist and was taking an extra part-time course at university to further her career. She had one son, Brendan, who was now three. She said her marriage was happy and settled, her husband considerate and "modern" in his views toward women. He was self-employed and would be taking paternity leave so as to help with the forthcoming child. She had nothing to complain about, but was filled with dread and fear. She had been unable to put the memory of the last birth and its aftermath behind her. I asked her to tell me what had happened.

Kathleen was a thorough organiser, so all was ready for the baby's arrival. Her husband, who came from a large happy family himself, was immensely excited, had helped enthusiastically to organise the nursery, sat in on prenatal classes, bought far more toys than was necessary. Both partners looked forward to the water birth, every detail of which had been carefully planned. Kathleen bade a temporary farewell to her colleagues at work and happily sat back to await the big event.

Sadly the labour went unexpectedly wrong. A life threatening situation developed and an emergency Caesarean section had to be performed. Kathleen was heavily sedated after she started having fits, while baby

Brendon was under intense observation in a special unit. Then there were tests and a further short stay in hospital. Once safely through the crisis, Kathleen returned home exhausted and bitterly disillusioned. She was used to getting things right, putting on a good show, doing what was required of her. To her horror, she felt nothing for the baby, try though she may to nurse him. He wouldn't take to the breast, yet her husband could soothe him with a bottle – another failure. Poor Kathleen turned away her friends, saying she was unwell, but in reality couldn't bear to let them see her maternal inadequacy. The medical team were supportive, but very overstretched. She put on such a convincing face that her Depression was minimised, the assumption being that time and rest would heal her. After all, her husband was such a rock for her; they should get through all right. How grateful she must be to have him.

Privately, Kathleen went through a hell of guilty hatred, for herself, for Ken her husband and for the baby. Between gritted teeth she bathed Brendan, slowly and precisely, step by step, as they'd been taught, watched, commented on and praised by her husband. But she longed to get it over with, and for cooing Ken to just shut up. She couldn't bear his encouragement; she shouldn't need it should she? She knew he could do the baby care ten times better, with more enthusiasm and with more love. As time went on she relied on him more and more to help with Brendan, yet hated him for being so able when she was so inept. "Once I virtually threw Brendan at him, when I was battling to get him inside a blue babygrow and Ken said he preferred the red one. Both of them were flattened against the wall as I stormed out in tears. I sat on the local swings and watched the night fall. The police found me there staring at the moon. I could have died of shame, realising, as they drove me home, that Ken must have told them what I'd done."

After this, Kathleen became docile, obedient, almost silent. Ken thought she was just very tired, brought in a part-time nurse for a few weeks and worked more at home so as to be available. There were no more violent scenes and Ken seemed pleased with her progress. She was getting the hang of it, he said; he'd known it would be all right in the end. What Kathleen never told him or anyone else was that suicidal thoughts were her only consolation for months. If the misery got any worse she could always end it all. Brendan would be well looked after, would almost certainly be better off without her.

It took more than a year and a return to work before she gradually recovered and could stop acting. "Will it all happen again?" she asked me, hand protectively across swollen belly, eyes rimmed with tears.

Alas this sad story is very typical of untreated postnatal Depression. For the purposes of this chapter though, we need to look at Kathleen in the round, not just her medical, psychiatric and hormonal state.

I asked about her personal history. She was the oldest of four sisters from a well-off family in southern Ireland. "Dad gave us the best of everything, private schools (nuns and all that), ponies, ballet. He bred race horses, travelled with them a lot, never home really. We had au pairs in the holidays, you know, foreign girls. . . Mum? Oh, for heaven's sake, our mum. She was mad for our local priest; they were always going on retreats or vigils or Lourdes or some place like that. Religion and a few nips of the old malt with her prayers, that was my mum."

Here was an intelligent, ambitious, extraverted woman who on the surface had led a privileged, cushioned life. However, despite the au pairs, she'd parented her younger sisters for as long as she could remember, playing with them, telling stories, comforting them, wiping their noses. She provided them with a loving maternal presence from the age of seven, as her own mother took to her bed after each child was born, and, on recovery, withdrew more and more into the church and her devotion to Father O'Connor.

As therapy continued, Kathleen, a scientist normally focussed on the busy outside world, began to look inside, reclaiming many desires and resentments long successfully suppressed. This was her first encounter with Depression and it had sapped all her confidence. No wonder she'd thought she was going to make an excellent mother herself, with all the practice she'd had. But what she'd not bargained for was the assault on her self-esteem when her body let her down and had to be handed over to the surgeon to be put right. We considered the prolonged sedation, how it might have somewhat addled her mind, disturbing that memory store. What of the carefree childhood, of which she'd been robbed but was now supposed to give to a demanding infant? Who had taken the trouble to emotionally mother *her*, while she cared for her sisters? What of her parents' negligence despite the creature comforts? Could her mother not have rallied round even for the birth of her first grandchild? ("Invite them? Whatever for? They aren't interested.") Proud of her independence, she'd not reckoned with the loneliness of giving birth without the comfort and sympathy of other women. In the sessions she was finally able to grieve for the mother she so longed for but had never had.

And what about her job and her studies? This was where Kathleen felt most alive, where she excelled and was appreciated. It was where her friendships were, where she could be herself without having to take care of anybody. Coming to a British university from Ireland had felt like coming home, not leaving it. Brendan's arrival had sent her right back to her roots. She was again a mother before she was ready to be a mother, her freedom snatched away. She'd wanted a baby, but more for Ken than herself. It had been too soon for her, but typically she'd thought she would be able to organise and manage it all.

Kathleen could now identify, appreciate and face the components of her Depression rather than just recoiling from the memory of months of bleakness and despair. She felt more compassion toward both her grown-up Self as a disillusioned and traumatised mother, and the lonely un-mothered child she herself had been. She had also to deal with the envy toward her husband who'd received in childhood all that she had been denied, as well as confronting her rivalry with him, now that he, not she, was the proficient, decisive one. I saw both of them for a few sessions to help Kathleen share with her husband the truth behind her former state and prepare them for the new baby. Their marriage had become strained after Brendan's birth and we wanted to avoid all that this time. I'm glad to say the second child was delivered safely and all went well.

The toddler (premature loss)

It's still sometimes assumed that a well-behaved toddler is a well-adjusted one, who's bound to become a good and happy citizen. A revolutionary series of films in the 1950s radically changed this view. Joyce and James Robertson unintrusively filmed toddlers who were in hospital for a variety of ordinary procedures. In those days parental visiting was severely restricted so as not to upset the child or interfere with the nurses' work. On the whole, the staff claimed, toddlers screamed for their mothers when they were first left behind on the ward, but soon settled in, quietened down and were content. These films show a very different story.

A child of two screams for her parents as they turn away from her cot on the unfamiliar ward and make for the door. When they fail to return she's bewildered but can tolerate their absence for a short time; she can still hope. She begins to gaze at the door. When they fail to return hour after hour, then day after day, she grows afraid, withdrawn, and finally abandons belief in their return. She becomes an automaton, compliant but showing no interest in anything – "such a good little girl" say the nurses. Watching the close-ups in the film, it's clear she has in fact lost all will to live. No point in tears, rage, protest. *No one will come.* This is despair. This is Depression.

Many studies were conducted afterwards, again and again demonstrating the damage done by a separation incomprehensible to the toddler. Later investigations of the same children showed a variety of behavioural problems, deep insecurities and alterations in their personality, most requiring treatment. Having viewed this evidence, the NHS changed its policy on visiting hours, thus preventing countless family tragedies. We owe a great debt to these early film makers.

The effects of separation, especially in the young but also in anyone facing a big transition in life, should never be underestimated. A history of separations never properly explained or negotiated by the one leaving, or never understood or accepted by the one who is left, should always alert us to the susceptibility of that person to Depression.

In contemporary western culture, one of the greatest developmental separations takes place toward the end of adolescence, ideally following a history of secure and predictable relations within a reasonably functional family. Leaving home, being wrenched from school pals, the first break-up with the first partner, the first failure or disillusionment at college or work that one's folks can't fix: these are painful but necessary lessons that we store up to aid us in the future when there are bigger unions and bigger separations waiting. We will by then have some resources to draw on. But the hospitalised two year old has none. It's important for any toddler's later mental health that moving from one life stage to another – weaning, potty training, nursery, or Mum just popping down the road to the shops – is facilitated by understanding adults.

It's not separation *per se* that does the damage, but the way it's mishandled by the actors involved, and by accumulated harm inflicted by previous badly managed and unhealed partings. Repeated unpredictable and/or unintelligible separations mean the child is conditioned to expect more betrayals and abandonments, and will build up coping strategies and defensive attitudes to protect themselves from the pain of these. These generally take the form of rebellion or withdrawal, manipulative, aggressive or clingy behaviours and an inability to keep relationships going. This "bad" behaviour can successfully disguise or ward off the underlying chronic Depression, which never receives the attention it so needs.

From home to school

Contrast the sad examples in the Robertsons' films with my first day at school. The developmental angle is clear. Here is a child entering a new realm, hearth and home no longer the only centre of her life; it's a huge stride into a more grown-up world. How her parents and her new teacher prepare her and actually hand her over from one domain into the other is critical. This is the current relationships angle. Then we have personal history to consider, whether the child's earlier experience has enabled her to feel sufficiently safe inside not to need the constant presence of Mum. As to the relationship to her own Self, does she feel she is up to the challenge, worthy of acceptance in this new environment?

So what happened to me? I'd never been to nursery nor had a sitter. My father was away during my early years and my older brother and sister were at school. I'd had my mother all to myself. I'd been closer to her than her own shadow. We looked out for each other, shared everything, confided in each other. I was scared stiff of going to school. How would my mum manage without me all day? And how was I to deal with other kids, for where and how I lived there were no pals to speak of, so no experience to draw on. Would they like me or hate me? Would I be clever enough for them, as some had already been to this nursery place – they might laugh at my ignorant ways. What would the teacher be like? Would she think me stupid or too highly strung (one of my mother's favourite descriptions of me)? Above all, would I "show her up", another cardinal sin? Might I cry, or displease the teacher, not be bright enough to understand what was going on? After all, this was School, grown-up land!

As it turned out, after initial shyness, trying to blend into the wallpaper, I found myself fascinated by, as well as nervous of, my surroundings. There were books, lots and lots of books. We had none at home. There were drums and tambourines and trumpets – music, like the radio, but real and touchable! And chalk, every colour of the rainbow. And heavens, the teacher was beautiful. She knew my name and where I lived and the date of my birthday. She took my hand, led me to the bookshelf and let me choose! There was just one proper lesson. The teacher wrote a great big ABC on the blackboard. I knew this, mentally hugged my older brother who at my insistence had taught me my letters. "Apple, Ball, Cat," I squealed. Phew, I was in with a chance.

By early afternoon though, anxiety kicked in. I had never in my life been away from my mum this long. Was she all right? Heavens, was *I* all right? I began to feel very shaky indeed, then fearful. Oh dear, what was this awful gnawing feeling in my tummy? It threatened at any minute to engulf my whole body. It was my first ever experience of *missing* of course, and I simply couldn't fathom it at all. It really frightened me. But the worst thing in the world, the most shaming thing, would be to *cause a fuss,* another of my mother's common utterances. Panic loomed.

My teacher intuited my distress, scooped me onto her knee and held me close. I was scandalised. No one but my mother ever did that! I perched on one of her thighs while she opened a big book onto her other and proceeded to read the whole class a lovely story. I could smell her face powder and watch her earrings wobble as she read aloud to us. I was in a sort of paradise. I had been chosen to sit on her knee, she had an arm round me, she must like me! But was I betraying my mother, all alone at home? Would she be upset if she knew about the face powder and the earrings? Should I stay true to her, ask to go back to my seat? No, it was too nice here. That's when I made my first irrevocable step away from my mother. I decided with much guilt and my first little thrill of independence, that I wouldn't tell her.

We can see that this child had a strong bond with her mother. Not once did it occur to her that her mum would fail to collect her. The day just felt so darn long. The teacher respected her shyness at first, then gradually brought her out of herself through her hunger to learn, experiment and express herself, until home was forgotten. Wisely, she stood in for Mum toward the end of the day as the stimulated but tired child began to feel guilt at having so enjoyed herself. Due to good previous history and intelligent here-and-now management in the classroom, a developmental milestone was achieved. Depression never got a look in!

Maggie's story (girl into woman)

I'll conclude this chapter by recounting Maggie's tale of adapting to a top drawer university after life on a dairy farm. Back at home for summer vacation, she came to see me in an agitated state, more like acute anxiety than any of the Depressions. She had just sacked a previous therapist who'd suggested she'd been the victim of incest. Shocked and outraged at the slur on her brother, she'd marched out and rushed home to her family, very upset. Her mother found my name as someone she hoped might calm her daughter while at the same time giving a second opinion on the self-diagnosed Depression.

Maggie had gone to the previous therapist on account of what she described as hopeless moods at university when she felt totally alone, unable to communicate with other students or join in any of the many activities she normally loved. She couldn't read or study and slept all day. These moods were interspersed with a busy and on the whole happy student life. She worked and played equally hard, "kept up", as she put it, with both the social and academic demands of student life.

We chatted about making friends, noisy smelly city life, which were the safest recreational drugs, how she missed the cows on the farm and the sunsets, what she felt about the planet and politics. I felt we were skirting round some secret or other but after her earlier experience of therapy I wasn't going to rush her. Soon the time to return to university for her second year came around. Her mood darkened but she felt more pressured "to get things sorted". I waited.

Then came "the secret". Clearly, she feared I would react badly but at the same time hoped I might shed some light on her worries. At college she was having dreams and masturbatory fantasies about her brother in Scotland. Horrified when these refused to go away, she thought her virginity might be responsible. Accordingly she "did the sex thing" to find that, though a bit embarrassing and clumsy, it had gone well and she was keen to try it again. It hadn't stopped the dreams though.

Herewith a bit of history that aids us make sense of all this. Maggie's father had been killed when she was three months old, crushed by farm machinery. Her brother Luke was ten at the time and "went into hiding" in his room for weeks. Granny took over Maggie and Luke's welfare for a few years while Maggie's mother turned to *her* brother, Maggie's uncle, who farmed nearby. Their farms were amalgamated and over the years built up into a successful enterprise. Maggie was fond of her uncle and loved her mum, but they were very busy people indeed. She and the introverted Luke turned to each other. They both revelled in the outdoors, in Nature, in animals, spending every available minute with each other, their other friends being secondary.

When she was fifteen, Luke was twenty-five and still working as an odd-job man round the local farms. Then he found a post as ferryman on a tiny boat hopping between Scottish islands and he moved to a ramshackle cottage there. She missed him greatly but she visited once or twice and they kept in contact.

Four years later she was swept into university life, anxious much of the time about her non-academic origins, whether she would be seen as a country bumpkin among all those toffs. She felt she could never quite speak their language, yet avoided other outsiders, as she called them, for fear this would just ostracise her further. She tried so hard to "join the pack". Then the black moods would hit and all she longed for was sleep. However, sexy dreams about her bother tormented her. Should she force herself to stay awake as long as possible, deny herself the post masturbatory relaxation she craved but at least enjoy a clear conscience? Why bother if the dreams still came? She couldn't stay awake all night could she? Was she just a pervert, twisted and evil? How could she look her friends in the eye carrying this awful secret?

She wasn't an innocent, she said: she knew about sex abuse; but what if deep down in her unconscious mind she herself wanted to be the abuser? Her brother would never in a million years have done or said anything inappropriate to her. He was an angel. It must be the other way round. She was disgusting, sick, abnormal. In the end she'd decided she needed treatment, for her brother's sake. Only to be told that he was the perverted one!

Now we see what was occurring. Stepping into a highly desired but somewhat alien and stressful world, a young girl on the cusp of womanhood yearns for the reassurance of home in the form of a departed brother whose years of physical proximity and unconditional love brought her so much tranquillity and self-assurance. In dreams he could be with her again. Sexually curious and active herself, it's hardly surprising that in sleep the competing need for adult sexual gratification and the child-like need for inner security got joined up, harmonised (the computer brain being no respecter of conscience or morals). Whenever the pressing demands within both the girl and the woman could not be satisfied in the real world another way to soothe herself had to be found, hence our old misunderstood friend, masturbation. It rescues and comforts, as long as it doesn't become an end in itself, an obsession. It was Maggie's needless anxiety, guilt and moral censure that was adding anxiety to her bad moods, not her evil nature.

By the time she arrived on my doorstep, Maggie's anxiety and self-recrimination had become more of a problem than her moodiness. In her short therapy she came to understand the battle with separation and loss that raged beneath her sunnier, more confident Self. She was able to differentiate between her dark moods to do with adjusting to university and what was a needless panic reaction to her longing for her brother. She started to communicate with Luke again, after having cut off communication for fear of contaminating him in some way. Unsurprisingly, as she did reconnect with him, the dreams lessened.

A note on anxiety

Anxiety frequently blends with, or comes before, symptoms of a Depression. A most debilitating state once it gets a hold on someone, anxiety does all the same have an upside. Hope hasn't vanished altogether, as in an established Depression. On the contrary, the sufferer is convinced there is hope for a good outcome, happiness even, if only they can only fend off some impending catastrophe, or find some miraculous guarantee of ongoing safety – a book, an ideology, a special person, a treatment. They can't rest till the way is cleared of all obstacles, for they anticipate disaster wherever they look. Before they dare use or enjoy life, they're attempting the impossible task of imprisoning safety in a strongbox.

In extreme cases of anxiety the internal drive to counteract constant dread is so relentless that it's a relief in the end to sink into Depression where the struggle can finally cease. Goodbye hope. But at least by collapsing this way the body that has been burning up all its adrenalin supplies can now get some rest and recuperation.

Acceptance of risk, of the impossibility of totally assured safety and of the inevitability of change doesn't protect us from harm and is scary; but it has to be better than the futile attempt to control everything that leads only to exhaustion and ultimately the desolation of Depression.

The state of anxiety itself was the real disaster for Maggie, not the fantasised one that had so terrified her. Maggie's fear that her dreams made her a monster and she'd poisoned her precious attachment to her brother disappeared with the acceptance and understanding of her competing desires that she acquired in therapy. Now able to appreciate the two way tug on her between the safe and sustaining past and the uncertain but invigorating present, she could contend better with her remaining dark moods. She could recognise them as part and parcel of maturation, a process far from completed as yet. But at least there was only one set of problems to face now. Symptoms can't be eradicated by magical guarantees but they are more easily borne, and often reduced, when some meaning can be found in them.

Chapter 6

The Psychological Perspective Continued – Two Counselling Stories

Unwrapping and sorting the bundle we call the Depressions, we've already identified the main types. So what about contributory factors over and above the chemical imbalance that could be either cause or consequence? Thus far we've registered: present compensatory or subverting relationships; the personal history of the sufferer that on top of their inherited propensities has rendered them resistant or vulnerable to the condition; ongoing relations with the person's own Self; and the importance of early loss and separation that can profoundly affect their later view of the world as a negative, untrustworthy place. We've also noted that when the person's Depression occurs at a significant stage in their life cycle, that stage and the disorder often have a reciprocal effect.

Let's now look in more detail. Those wanting to better understand a specific episode happening before their eyes or within themselves need to consider and assess all the above, but may also need to incorporate other features frequently noted by the professionals, that dominate some Depressions. For example there are Depressions coloured by *denial and avoidance*, by *abuse and trauma*, by *hate*, and by their *function* (they are fulfilling a purpose that the sufferer is unaware of). As we shall see from the illustrations to come, these are all embedded in a set of highly pertinent emotional attachments which throw much light on why and how the Depression has appeared now rather than at some other time. "Why now?" is a key question to ask when appraising a disordered mood.

We should not forget however, that the predominantly genetic and cyclical kinds don't conform to contextual dictates and can arise any time, anywhere. There may or may not be triggers of course, but breast-beating by relatives and partners wondering if it could be all their fault has no place here. A correctly diagnosed illness of this sort can materialise out of the blue irrespective of past and present relationships or external events. No one is to blame. To be useful "all you need is love", as the song goes – and patience.

Much of the forthcoming material concerns little 'd' depression, so let's do a brief recap. Little 'd' depression needs intervention wherever possible and is a serious but not life-threatening matter, or one that renders the person entirely unable to cope with the basics of everyday living. In my experience this is the kind of mood state that benefits most from talking therapy, though help has to be voluntarily accepted and often isn't! Threat of divorce, withdrawal of funds, bribery and guilt-tripping by well-meaning relatives don't help the therapist to do their work. Therapy is a partnership, a dual responsibility. It's a conversation, shared detective work, an alliance, not an imposition. You can't do good therapy *to* a person, only *with* them.

This kind of low mood varies in degree and over time, like any other. Jo, the cyclothymic BT engineer, described his own down periods neatly with little diagrams of eclipses that he sketched for me each week, once he saw I was interested in his moods as well as his women.

Jo's Cyclothymia

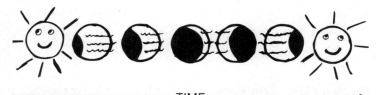

TIME

His complete sequence took around six or seven weeks, the happy (at their peak a bit too happy?) intervals lasting just less than the sad ones. He was at pains to emphasise that the black bits on the diagram meant dead: as impossible to shift as trying to move the real sun sideways to avoid a real eclipsing shadow. But the rest of him operated more or less as usual, indeed went through various ordinary minor moods depending on what was happening at the time, hence the wiggly bits passing over the sun's non affected parts. These represent cloud cover, rain and other vagaries of psychological "weather". He could drive his van, visit homes and chat to customers, but in the down times it was an effort, at the worst times a huge, draining effort, as so much of the energy-giving light was cut off by the dead bits. Only when he let himself relax did his close mates notice the fatigue and pessimism behind his usual cheery façade.

Used in every day conversation, "depression" means a gloomy outlook or an expression of disappointment and sadness in reaction to some unwelcome occurrence, but doesn't refer to any part of the individual as dead. From the inside these two experiences are qualitatively different. The one may need a pal, a stiff drink, a good sleep or a holiday. The other could use a therapist.

Depression coloured by denial/avoidance

James's story

"My GP tells me I have retirement-related depression and won't give me pills till I've tried talking therapy."

James was a sixty-five year old architect, slim, beautifully turned out in fashionable chinos and cashmere sweater, designer socks. Shoulders drooped, hands hanging between his knees, he shook his well coiffured head, baffled.

"How can I be depressed? I'm well off, luxury Kensington house, member of the top clubs – though money shouldn't matter of course. The practice I set up aeons ago is now one of the best in London – the most exclusive clients, foreign potentates, rock stars, the lot. But we've also done masses for local councils and for charity over the years – I'm really proud of all that. We've been, you know, honourable, decent. I'm going to miss my partners when I go. . . I'm choosing to retire you know, not being forced or anything. I want to do new things, time to move on, as they say."

He sighed, then straightened up as if to fight his weariness.

"Best of all I'm off to Africa on a United Nations advisory team soon, helping rebuild towns and villages decimated by years of tribal warfare. Purely voluntary basis of course, have to do my bit, give something back."

"You say best of all, but don't look too pleased about it. . ."

"There's the rub. It *was* a big deal for me. I was so flattered to be asked, had masses of ideas for the project. Then, unaccountably, I slumped. I'm still keen to go; it's not the project's fault. It's me. Am I getting old or ill, or what? I'm tired all the time but wake at four in the morning and can't get back to sleep. . . . . Thoughts whirling about? No, nothing like that; just, well, a sort of apathy, a sense of, well, pointlessness. I carry on at work though I delegate more than usual, take longer breaks. As a senior partner that's one of my privileges, but not one I normally use. It's appalling. I just can't be bothered. I am not *myself.*"

This certainly sounded like a little 'd' depression, but why? Neither his blood tests nor his physical examination had shown anything awry and he was disappointed he'd not been given vitamins or some kind of tonic. We agreed the whole thing was puzzling but arranged to meet again to try and tease things out.

I realised later how James had kept aside every fact salient to his state of mind in that first session. This was not deliberate. His brain had been working hard behind the scenes to avoid matters too painful to confront, while he worriedly discussed his symptoms. He was *in denial.*

This is what gradually surfaced in subsequent meetings. He'd been divorced aged thirty, when the wife that had been more his parents' choice than his left him for someone else. Since then he'd lived happily alone, his aesthetic flair making him fussy about standards – "confirmed bachelor, stuck in my ways". The building up of his practice and his love for fine art became his twin passions in life and overall he'd been content. At my prompting he admitted to only one "sort of" love affair.

One day he'd been on site inspecting one of his firm's ventures when a man just ahead of him was knocked down by a plank swinging from machinery. Along with others, he rushed to the rescue. The injured plasterer sought out James after the accident, and James agreed to meet him, fearing his firm may be about to be sued or blackmailed. What actually transpired was the uncovering of his true nature in a thrilling but terrifying night of intense sex. Thus began a thirty year, secret homosexual relationship that was now under threat.

James's father was a Hertfordshire C. of E. vicar, his mum a loving but meek wife and indulgent mother. James was a practising Christian, more out of habit and affection than deep belief, but had now to face his sexual orientation and what to do and think about it. "My parents would never have got over it, though they'd have said all the right, tolerant things. No, I couldn't bear it. And what about my friends, my colleagues, my club, my public face – all those charitable committees? No no, impossible. . . Yes, I know this is the nineteen nineties and who cares, but, well, it was a long time ago. And we were so *different.* How was I to go to the opera with a plasterer who never listened to anything but Radio One, whose idea of culinary refinement was a burger and chips? The Mona Lisa was the only painting he'd ever heard of. Snobby maybe, but it was the truth. I was half exhilarated and half ashamed by what we did. But it couldn't go on, could it?"

But it did go on. Rather than struggle internally with the implications of his homosexuality, decide whether to come out or not, what, if anything, to change about the way he lived, he simply *avoided* the whole conflict, disassociated himself from it. He continued with his usual successful and busy life, engaging in charity and then political enterprises that his other persona must never be allowed to sully. Twice, sometimes three times a year, he and Peter Plasterer, as he called his partner, made assignations to meet up in some Mediterranean hideaway for a week or two's holiday.

Peter turned out to be rather intelligent, full of ideas and argument about life, even if his considerable but rather cynical wisdom had been acquired on the rougher streets of London. His grab-it-while-you-can philosophy and gritty humour shocked then liberated much of James's harsh conscience as they became friends as well as lovers. A conventional partnership was for James out of the question though. Peter raised it but once, and never again. Both kept the myth going that this was just something "on the side", "a bit of naughty", purely for fun and relaxation.

Now, thirty years on, James had written to Peter – he distrusted phones for his private communications – and told him about the retirement plan that would keep him abroad for at least a year. There was no possibility of visits and anyway it was a Muslim country – no booze and no gay sex, so Peter wouldn't care for it at all. Also there must be no scandal, given the whole thing was backed by a subsidiary of the United Nations. I suspected he was trying one last time to put his secret life behind him, still very scared his name and his lifelong achievements could be tarnished or destroyed. The unnecessary retirement and flight to Africa seemed a contrivance, a geographical way out of the conflict between his "better" public Self and his disapproved of private Self. The nearer he got to a knighthood the more acute the conflict became, along with the pressure to resolve it.

To his astonishment, Peter wrote back saying he was fed up of being James's bit of totty, a Big Cheese's toy boy, something to be just picked up and thrown away twice a year. On and on the letter went. "Must have been drunk as a skunk," said James in some distaste. It was soon followed by a more sober letter saying he'd been unable to work due to a back problem and that being pinned flat to the floor on painkillers had given him time for thought. He had decided to end what he called the "non relationship" once and for all. He was tired of being messed about. He hinted that there was someone more appreciative of him on the horizon.

As ever, James resorted to denial and avoidance. Ending things was quite convenient really. His reputation would be secure and he was going to be away for a year anyway, so missing Peter was irrelevant. He pushed to one side his stab of concern about that back problem: Peter knew how to take care of himself. Jealous feelings were also dismissed. In

Africa he wouldn't have time for such immature nonsense. But soon after, that little 'd' depression had crept upon him.

James had avoided facing conflict all his life: with his wife, parents, colleagues and his own sexuality, so it might be expected that he would deal with his disordered mood in the same manner. Rather than look at his symptoms from the inside, he opted to ask for drugs, which his doctor wisely declined to prescribe.

The turning point in therapy came when, in one of James's more pensive moments, I said "You truly love Peter, I think, and he loves you." Tears fell for the first time in his life. Amazingly, he'd never admitted this to himself, and not once had it crossed his mind to link his present symptoms with his impending loss.

The two men did arrange to meet for talks at James's instigation, but therapy finished before their relationship was finally settled. The last thing I heard was that the Africa trip had been postponed.

Depression coloured by hate

Lars's story

Lars was Norwegian, an elderly lecturer in Scandinavian literature. He came into therapy after a major breakdown, a definite big 'D' involving hospitalisation. He was now in the closing period of recovery and I judged him ready for therapeutic work. He was still low, but keen to understand what had happened to him and why, in the hope that future attacks might be prevented.

Lars grew up in Norway, deeply attached to his mother and with little feeling either way for his largely absent father. His mother belonged to a religious sect that believed in unquestioning love of others, prayer, a healthy lifestyle and self-control in order to find union with God. All ailments, physical and mental, arose out of shortcomings in these areas and could only be "treated" by a rebalancing of them. Doctors and blood transfusions went against this doctrine and so his mother's cancer was allowed to take its course until she died. She accepted her illness as divine judgement and serenely anticipated her meeting with her Maker, as the terrified Lars, sixteen years old, looked on. He couldn't rage at cruel Fate as a natural part of his grief, for he'd been imbued with the notion that rage and hate were forbidden and wicked.

A year later his father married again. Lars found this unbearable and left home to live with his mates, working as a waiter till he could get to England and university. Once employed here, he never returned to Norway. He married a fellow student whom he had accidentally made pregnant, but she was very unstable and had several breakdowns, finally taking her own life when their little girl Olga was only three. From that moment on, Lars dedicated his whole life to keeping his child safe. He never married again, burying himself in his books and writing learned papers. He stayed home as much as possible, watching over Olga, and so failed to make any lasting friendships. His university colleagues and students must have found him somewhat eccentric.

Lars had hoped his daughter would follow in his academic footsteps, might even become a better writer than he, more celebrated, admired across the world: a father can dream, surely? All that Olga yearned for however were dolls, Wendy houses, pretty clothes and her little friends. She must have all that her heart desires thought Lars, and surrendered, providing everything she demanded.

Like her dead mother, Olga became pregnant before she was out of her teens. She married the father of her child, who graduated from his business studies course and rapidly rose to area manager in a retail chain. They had another child very soon and Olga seemed perfectly content. She organised Lars, turned him into the ideal granddad, marking up his calendar so he'd be sure to visit the children at set times to play with them or put them to bed, while she prepared her husband's lavish dinners or entertained her friends. His own research took second place. When Olga and her family moved to a bigger house Lars moved as well, a few streets away. He just needed to be near her and she was delighted with the arrangement. They met almost daily. Relations between the two men however, were distinctly cool.

Lars chided himself for selfishness when Olga told him, hand in hand with her husband, both glowing with pride, that she was pregnant again. All he felt was sadness, that she was moving further from him, though he smiled and congratulated them, opened the champagne. When the child was only months old Olga's husband was again promoted and was to be transferred to New York. She begged not to be separated from her father, but was eventually persuaded to go by her husband, who for the first time laid down the law rather, demanding to know where her priorities lay. She promised Lars she would fly over whenever she could; there'd be much more money now. Lars said (and believed) that all he wanted was for her to be happy. Of course she must go. He helped her with all the preparations and the selling of their house, went on babysitting.

Lars's growing sense of sadness deteriorated into something much more serious. He lost weight, couldn't concentrate, took sick leave, stayed in bed staring at the walls for hours, and was eventually admitted to an acute psychiatric ward. Olga refused to leave his side and her husband's job was given to someone else. He stood by her but was sullen and resentful. The marriage became strained and the children grew fractious and unmanageable under the care of a kind but despised private nanny, while Olga herself regularly broke down in tears during the hospital visits, seeing her father so broken.

Lars was overcome with guilt and self-loathing, couldn't bear the thought that his illness had been instrumental in spoiling his daughter's life, the life he'd sworn to preserve and protect no matter the cost to him. He must free her from all this. He saved each dose of the medication the nurses gave him and then took the lot in one go. Fortunately he was found unconscious in the toilet, and after that he was given ECT.

Given the title of this section of the chapter, you will know what has happened here. A young boy conditioned never to hate doesn't know how to feel it when such an emotional reaction would have been appropriate and could have even prevented mental illness later on. Hate was driven underground over and over again. In therapy, after a lengthy and guilt-laden struggle, Lars accessed his hatred of his mother's religious elders, of his father for forgetting his mother so soon, his wife for her self-murder when Olga so badly needed her, and finally his long buried hatred of Olga's husband; for it was he who had stolen his only remaining reason for living, his treasured daughter.

Lars came to see how the Depression that almost killed him had served to prevent his daughter from leaving him (thus fulfilling his unconscious wishes whilst allowing him to go on believing he wanted her happiness above all else). Having confronted this unsavoury truth he worried about getting ill again every time a new abandonment loomed. This in turn forced him to take on board his own

dependency on Olga rather than seeing his life in terms
of her dependency on him. In order to please and protect
her at first, but later to fill his own barren existence, he'd
forfeited any independent life of his own.

These revelations disheartened him but sadness is not an
illness. In the end it motivated him to redirect his attention
away from his recent terrifying illness toward his future
health, perhaps a future without his daughter. For the
saddest realisation of all was that it was time to loosen the
bonds, to let her go.

A note on hate

Most of us opt for a decent, ethical world of kindness
and love, so find the notion of hate abhorrent or sinful,
especially as there is rarely any justification for it if we can
be open minded and fair. Was not Lars's mother entitled
to her beliefs, his father to fall in love again, his poorly wife
to end her mental agony, Olga's husband to take her to a
brighter future? But hate obeys no rules. It's a tool in our
emotional survival kit that like other tools can kill or cure,
make safe or destroy. It's neither intrinsically good nor bad,
it just *is*. What we do with it is what matters!

Denying and avoiding hate leads to situations like Lars's,
where only major illness can come to the rescue, but what
a price to pay to get what we think we need. Better surely

to first recognise hate, then puzzle out the reasons for it, before controlling the impulses it's driving us to lest we regret them later. It may be offensive and unacceptable to our better nature to acknowledge hate, but if tabooed it's a menace to mental health. I'm not saying hate is good for us, but wrestling honestly with it makes us a healthier person than the one whose hate is repudiated only to worm itself into unwholesome relationships. Unexpressed lifelong hate coupled with major unprocessed losses led Lars into a co-dependent attachment to his daughter, which ultimately helped neither of them.

During our conversations Lars came to see how suicide is sometimes homicide in disguise. His hatred was focussed not only on Olga's husband, but on them as a unit, a hated couple breeding an alien family that threatened him with yet another cruel separation, this time from the only relationship in his life that mattered. He could kill them. But Olga was a conspirator in this defection. How could he murder her? His tortured mind transposed his hatred into "I will not kill you Olga, because I love you. Instead I will turn my *evil* (mother's legacy) hatred onto myself, to save you." But there was a sting in the tail: "*Then you'll be sorry.*" At a conscious level, Lars only ever had the welfare of his daughter at heart, but now at last he saw the undercurrent of his fury at her betrayal and desertion, which so echoed all the others.

For as long as he could remember, Lars's mother's teachings disavowed anger and hatred in any form, so he was totally unequipped to deal with his true feelings. The mind has many subterranean operations, one of which is to keep its owner on good terms with their Self, so murderous thoughts and impulses which would shame and horrify the "good" Self must be sunk without trace. If they are so strong they threaten to resurface, as with Lars, then the whole system must be shut down – big 'D'!

If hatred was more often recognised at source, then shared in a non-judgemental environment, revulsion and self-blame would be neutralised by understanding and many Depressions ameliorated or prevented.

A note on anger

By the time Lars terminated his therapy he felt more confident about identifying early warning signs and tackling them before they turned into illness, After all, he'd never had a breakdown before, though he added: "I see now, how all my life this one has been waiting to happen." His last task was to confront his daughter's role in all this – role, not fault. She'd exploited to the hilt (been trained to it!) the part of Little Princess, waltzing round her newly designed kitchen or off to buy new clothes while he put his work on hold to look after the children or chauffeur her while her husband was at work. He'd been at her beck and call for years.

"Bloody hell fire!" he burst out toward the end of his therapy. "I've been so bloody angry with her for so flaming long, and I never knew it! Daren't see it lest I lose her. She's run me ragged all her life, the little bitch." This eruption freed him to start examining his compliance, the surrender of his own needs to hers, which was not always so altruistic as it appeared. She *must* love him back, she *owed* it to him. How dare she just up sticks for New York? Once he accepted how he'd swallowed his anger at and disappointment in her for years, he could begin to explore the reasons why, rather than negatively judging these feelings in his mothers' prohibitive terms. His own demand for a return on his emotional investment in Olga stood revealed. This wasn't easy to face but it finally helped extricate him from the unhealthier side of this otherwise loving attachment.

Anger, like hate, is a given part of our nature as *homo sapiens.* Alongside hate, it has a tendency to be denied, avoided, sublimated into sport, re-directed at conveniently distant politicians, or drowned in alcohol. As with hate, anger may be ugly and destructive, but, as Lars discovered, it can also liberate, and, in tandem with insight, actually heal. Anger itself is not morally bad or good – it's just a set of responses available to us – but many of our ethical systems attribute a negative value to it. Depressions serve to damp down or even kill bodily and emotional arousal that could end up in angry expression, and thus we can stay on good terms with our Self, occupy the high moral ground.

We should remember though that anger is a mobiliser and Depression a stultifier. I know which I would rather wrestle with.

A woman in one of Olga Tokarczuk's novels discovers a photograph showing her two missing dogs, shot dead by hunters.

My body tensed, I was ready to do battle. My head began to spin, and a dismal wailing rose in my ears, a roar, as if from over the horizon an army of thousands was approaching – voices, the clank of iron, the creek of wheels in the distance. Anger makes the mind clear and decisive, able to see more. It sweeps up other emotions and takes control of the body. Without a doubt Anger is the source of all wisdom, for anger has the power to exceed any limits.

This is the kind of cleansing catharsis that Lars experienced upon his sudden confrontation with his true feelings toward his manipulative daughter. This was no ordinary bit of crossness. Frightening to witness, it nonetheless marked the start of his constructive separation from her and the repair of his self-regard.

Some functions of the Depressions

Lars's case demonstrates some of the hidden functions performed by a Depression. It can be used by the mind as a painkiller, an anaesthetic; it can control the actions and decisions of others without the sufferer's conscious intent. (Lars's mind was prepared to put up with illness if it kept his daughter home.) It can freeze internal conflict, avoid or delay having to come down on one side or the other of ambivalent feelings; it can paralyse the agonies of conscience; it can neutralise hate by turning it against the Self; it can numb emotions that the sufferer would roundly denounce if they were allowed to break through. In a family one person can be "elected" to bear all its members' denied unmanageable sadnesses while the rest get off scot-free. In marriage it can be deployed (unconsciously of course) to circumvent facing the end, or to force the partner into dealing with what they have long been side-stepping. Some couples share Depression between them: as one goes up, the other comes down, and thus the relationship is kept regulated and intact without either of them being aware of what's going on.

A note on trauma

In the case of recent abuse or trauma, shock and a degree of withdrawal while the incident is internally processed is of course to be expected. Indeed, the absence of such a response would indicate a massive blocking out defence mechanism almost guaranteed to produce later consequences – what we diagnose these days as post-traumatic stress disorder. However, some victims fail to heal with time and develop a deep emotional and physical sense of insecurity that morphs into a Depression. Their deadness at least protects them from having to relive the horror of the event day after day, of having to undergo the threat of disintegration to that carefully constructed and reasonably confident Self they used to enjoy before it was cruelly stolen from them.

Some Depressions (by no means all!) are a necessary time-buying and pain suppressant manoeuvre of the mind. Its purpose is to give an injured Self space, time and rest so as to re-organise and re-establish itself before tentatively re-engaging with the world. Too hasty intervention with psychological "techniques" and thought exercises risks re-traumatising the person, while too hasty a drug prescription may hinder any natural recovery resources still in play, even if not yet evident. Skilled assessment and pacing is critical.

The extent to which a traumatised victim recovers depends a good deal upon the sturdiness of their sense of Self predating the trauma. A good enough childhood with not too much exposure to loss, separation and disappointment, but sufficient duress to inoculate the burgeoning Self against further blows from fate, helps us metabolise new trauma. Those whose childhood lacked continuity and stability and who were unable to compensate themselves via other relationships find it very hard to reinstate a badly shaken sense of Self. In these instances the new traumatic event tears open old wounds, reviving the primal fear of not being able to cope with or even psychologically survive what is happening to them. Flashbacks can be so terrifying in post-traumatic stress that a temporary mind-death in the form of one of the Depressions is more tolerable.

This cushioning function in some of the Depressions can be seen as one of the mind's ways to help us survive, although, paradoxically, when it goes to extremes, as in uni- and bipolar, it can kill us. Even in less severe little 'd' depression, creativity, sociability and decision making is impoverished; it's a solution of last resort.

Some major Depressions appear not to have any function at all, but present as if the chemistry has just decided to go haywire, as in the compulsively ruminative type. Every waking moment the sufferer overhauls real or imagined faults and wrongdoing, regrets and if-onlys, putting themselves on trial and finding themselves guilty. Their mind is full of self-accusation and self-blame. Then we see the opposite type, where it looks to the observer as if the person's mind is empty, that blank despair has taken over, the person is almost in stupor.

When a Depression of any kind gets stuck, drags on with no variation; when it seems never to have function or meaning for the person enduring it or the people trying to help them, it's time to consider medication. If successful and the mood begins to lift sufficient for the sufferer to take an interest in what they are going through, counselling along with medication can very helpful. However, some people prefer to sit it out, wait for recovery, then put the whole horrible experience behind them. It's their choice.

As with anger and hate, the capacity for Depression is built in to us: there is no obligatory opprobrium or merit attached to it unless we deem it so. Therefore it behoves us to understand and do business with it rather than vainly trying to outlaw it or marginalise sufferers as weird or weak and certainly not like us!

Chapter 7

Treatments for the Depressions

The standard approach to all types of this diagnosis is drugs and/or talking therapies, but quality treatment is much more complex than that. We've already seen how the Depressions are embedded in, affect and are affected by marriages, families, the workplace and the sufferer's friends. These people are the repositories of all the hope temporarily abandoned by the impaired person, and carry it for them till they are better. To that end they can be seen as part of the treatment. No drug can manufacture love and loyalty and no talking therapy can produce miracles or be available round the clock. It has to be admitted though that some families are damaging and some sufferers have no close attachments to fall back on in times of trouble: these are the ones most at risk. It should also go on record that family and friends are not substitutes for therapists and doctors and can't be expected to act in a saintly manner at all times: living with a person whose attitude to everything is negative, who is unmotivated and frequently unwashed, can be very draining. The supporting responsibilities need to be shared among loved ones if secondary casualties are to be avoided. All too often it falls to one family member or partner to do all the caring work. Who supports them?

Effective help starts with a treatment *plan*, worked out at the time of diagnosis *with* the patient, not foisted upon them. It takes into account, not only their views on and knowledge about medication and counselling, but also details such as how they are to spend their day if they're not for the moment able to work. Are they too unwell or just well enough for occupation, distraction and fresh social contact in the form of day provision in the NHS or through charities? Are there support groups they may (or may not!) be willing to attend? Do they belong to a church, club or other organisation that might welcome involvement? Who is to deal with the employer to ensure their comfortable reinstatement when the time comes? Along with the sufferer, who is to monitor the pill-taking, watching for signs indicating increase or decrease of medication? Who is to ensure proper food, sleep, hygiene? Who is to keep an eye on their admin – bills, banking and so on?

A GP assessing the risk of self-harm needs to be aware of who is around in the background, able to cope at critical moments in the course of the Depression. Who does the person trust most, and who least? Some delicate exploring of family and couple dynamics can do a lot to prevent a worsening of symptoms. In short, the patient's Depression doesn't exist in a vacuum or disappear when they leave the surgery. Where possible, the doctor can make their own life easier, as well as their patient's, by working out together how home life is to be managed.

If talking therapy is recommended, then the plan should cover what particular kind would best suit the person – one size does not fit all, and sadly NHS provision is so limited that the individual may have to pay in order to get what is best for them. When would be the best time to start – alongside medication, after medication starts to work, without medication but keep a watching brief? Whenever it commences, follow-up appointments in the surgery give encouragement and something to look forward to, as recovery is jointly noted, medication adjusted, *human contact sustained*. Having lost faith in themself for the duration of the episode, it's essential that the patient is reassured that they still matter. This is part of the treatment itself, not just kindness.

I will summarise here the main sorts of medication available and the different types of talking therapy on offer. There is more detailed information easily accessible online. I suggest you start with the NHS and MIND websites. Next I will take two cases diagnosed as Depression from a GP surgery where I worked as resident counsellor, describing both the treatment and the influential relationships surrounding the patient. Some people given this label don't see themselves as ill and feel patronised or infantilised by the terms "patient", "illness" and "Depression". It's a great shame that such stigma remains. No offence or undermining is intended in this book, but when discussing events that transpire in a general practice surgery, medical terms seem the appropriate language to use.

Drugs

Antidepressants

The most commonly prescribed antidepressants these days are the SSRIs (Selective Serotonin Reuptake Inhibitors). This group are the most recently developed and have the least side effects. Antidepressants do not make you happy (high), but by increasing the flow of serotonin round the brain (it is claimed) aim to gradually lift mood from the doldrums. They don't resolve painful problems underlying the Depression. Effects are very individual and sometimes you have to experiment with more than one drug in the group before finding one that suits. Some people feel better quickly whilst a few others report no benefit. Yet others describe disturbing reactions that make them stop the drug as soon as they have started – dizziness or talking too fast, or feeling impulsive or drunk, for example. Mostly though, there is a bit of disappointment that nothing much happens for a while. SSNRIs are similar but have the added ingredient of the hormone noradrenaline. There is no doubt many feel a mood lift eventually with either of these groups but there is no exact explanation for this as yet, other than the brain's own serotonin being a part of the complex chemical picture.

What we do know from long experience is that the older tricyclics and MAOIs (MonoAminOxidase Inhibitors), which are still prescribed when SSRIs fail, have stronger side effects and can be lethal in overdose. With these older drugs it's very important to know about possible side effects (read the leaflet!) and to take these only under regular medical monitoring. I would strongly advise against self-medication and the purchasing of drugs on the internet. These are powerful chemicals that act on other bodily systems, not just mood: they are not sweeties and are not for recreation unless your idea of fun is dicing with danger.

And just to state the obvious: keep out of the reach of children!

There exists a powerful lobby who questions the validity of the serotonin "myth" and feels strongly about the whole pharmaceutical industry marketing these products. Speaking as a therapist rather than scientist or chemist, all I can say is that I have seen cases where in my opinion drugs should never have been prescribed, and others where people have been brought back from the brink thanks to their medication which raised their spirits enough to motivate them to use other agencies to help them recover.

There is much controversy in this area and you may wish to consult *Let Them Eat Prozac* by professor David Healy of Bangor University (NYU Press, 2006) to gain a wider view than I present here.

Antipsychotics (sometimes called *neuroleptics*)

Antipsychotics are mainly used for severe Depression, as well as other mental illnesses like schizophrenia and mania. They don't stop all delusions and hallucinations so don't cure the illness, but persons taking them report that they grow less and less bothered by these symptoms. The neural connection between experiencing them and wanting to act on them is chemically severed. Malevolent voices may remain in the person's head but there is little motivation to act on the voices' instructions. Again there are side effects which need careful supervision.

There are specific drugs for long term use in bipolar, that flatten the high-low mood swings. They can produce a high toxicity level if not regularly monitored with blood tests. Many people with bipolar and other psychotic illnesses are maintained most of the time in good health and lead normal lives with these drugs, without anyone in the vicinity realising what they have to contend with. Employers need to be sympathetic to the medical requirement for check-up appointments.

Others

Some antidepressants have a built-in anti-anxiety factor so that drugs such as the once notorious Valium are prescribed much less often. As with various other tranquillisers of the benzodiazepine group, and with sedatives for sleeping too, these drugs become addictive when taken over long periods. However, in acute crisis

many of them can be very helpful indeed, so don't
rule them out. They render the brain less sensitive to
stimulation so can quickly calm you down. A few nights
with a sedative can restore disturbed sleep habits without
causing any harm, but underlying causes need attention to
avoid the person becoming dependent on the "quick fix".

Beta blockers

Beta blockers block the adrenaline rush that comes when
you are suddenly very anxious. If you can't talk yourself
down or be talked down by a pal, they are useful for
temporary exam nerves and driving tests, being pretty
mild in their effects (unless there are pre-existing adverse
medical conditions).

HRT (hormone replacement therapy)

HRT is used for low or fluctuating moods in menopausal
women, as well as for physical symptoms, with good
results for some and not others. Any cancer risks should
be discussed with your doctor. It's a controversial and
complicated field.

ECT (electro convulsive therapy, or electroplexy)

In ECT, after a muscle relaxant and light anaesthetic is
injected, a gadget rather like a headphone set is applied
to the temples and a carefully measured electric current
passed through the brain, mimicking an epileptic fit
("mimicking" because the muscle relaxant makes the
convulsions barely visible). Some confusion may be

experienced afterwards but usually soon clears up. A course of treatments may be given at varying intervals over several weeks. This technique is now very safe, not nearly so barbaric as many imagine. Usually deployed as a last resort, it has saved the lives of many people with suicidal Depression who have failed to respond to antidepressants. And let's be honest about this – no one knows *exactly* why antidepressants work and why the same drug that's right for one is hopeless for another. Research marches on but there are as many unanswered questions in the chemical field as there are in the neurological one.

Other brain stimulation techniques are being experimented with currently. TMS (transcranial magnetic stimulation) deploys a curved bit of apparatus (a bit like a horseshoe) generating a magnetic field that does something similar to but weaker than ECT. It's held over the head of the subject. There's no need for anaesthesia but you have to have several treatments a week for some weeks. Neurotechnology is also coming on apace, trying out brain implants (the same concept as heart pacemakers) that might perform the same function of shaking up mood by electrically exciting the brain. Who knows, by the time this book is published these may be available to the general public. (Should we be pleased or horrified? And if we don't suffer from severe Depression ourselves, who are we to judge?) For the moment results are inconclusive but as far as I am aware no one has been hurt in the course of research.

The talking therapies

These fall into four main groups, CBT (Cognitive Behavioural Therapy), psychodynamic, humanistic and integrative, each of these having many subgroups and specialisms within them, making the field very complicated for the would-be client.

CBT (Cognitive Behavioural Therapy)

CBT trains you to be aware of how (rather than what) you think, and to recognise the modes of behaviour and the attitudinal positions you habitually adopt under given circumstances. If these are proving counterproductive, alternatives can be suggested and practised. You'll be given mental or practical "exercises" to do in your own time, may be asked to keep records of moods and reactions to certain events and to insert opposing or challenging thoughts and behaviours to them when they next appear. Homework results are fed back to the practitioner (or workshop group) and fresh tasks are then fine-tuned to suit your personal needs. You should find yourself noticing and questioning fixed viewpoints on life and your own Self, cultivating better social skills, and learning a few techniques for controlling and distracting yourself from anxiety and sinking mood. This usually short term approach is rooted in the present and doesn't concern itself with early development.

Humanistic therapy

The *humanistic* counsellor follows wherever the client needs to go in the session, offering warmth, empathy and respect. They refrain from advice or judgement. They don't pursue the past life of their client but will accompany them if that is where they wish to explore. They don't give advice or suggest hidden meanings. This counselling is essentially client-led, the emphasis being on the healing nature of an authentic relationship rather than administered techniques.

Psychodynamic Therapy

The *psychodynamic* approach is similar in most respects to that of the humanistic one, except that the authentic relationship that grows between therapist and client is seen not only as an end in itself, but also as a tool for shared investigation of the client's past experiences that are brought *unconsciously* into their current relationships, including the one with the therapist sometimes. Because of its depth and the revisiting of painful times for the client, this approach requires careful pacing and delicate handling, so on the whole takes more time and regular meetings with the therapist.

Integrative Therapy

The *integrative* counsellor aims to make a synthesis of all these "schools", but can't be an expert in all of them: that's just not possible. They will almost certainly lean in one of the above directions more than the others and it may prove worth your while to find out which.

It should not need saying, but I'll say it anyway. Check your counsellor/therapist is fully qualified and accredited. Even that is no guarantee. If you don't get on with them, whatever their credentials, leave!

Tales from the GP's surgery

Frank's story

Frank's wife Mary came to see her doctor and poured out her troubles which he later relayed to me. Frank refused to see the doctor himself, being "ridiculously prejudiced" against the entire medical profession, so she'd come on his behalf. "He mooches about all day, miserable as sin, chuntering on about how awful everything is, not looking after himself, sleeping all hours. He's depressed, I reckon, and told him so, but he won't have it. Only thing he can still do is the sex, cuddles up like a baby and wants it all the time. Now I've as much red blood in my veins as the next woman, and I comfort him when I can; but who wants sex with such a moany, scruffy old bugger? I tell you, I'm at my wits' end; he won't listen to me. I have to do everything about the place while he sits muttering to himself. I just can't take it any more".

Mary and the GP cooked up a plot. Mary would tell Frank he needn't see the doctor right away. There was an elderly counsellor lady, sweet, wouldn't harm a fly (I cringed at the description) who would listen to him – no pills, no trick cyclists, just listening. No harm in just talking, was there? And the trip out would do him good, bit of fresh air.

The surgery offered up to ten sessions of counselling. In his first one a dishevelled Frank stared at the floor, mumbling in monotone about the uselessness of everything, from potholes that never got filled to psycho dictators, from the celebrity-mad kids of today to the rape of the planet, all without once making eye contact. Eventually I interrupted the gloom with a few questions.

I gathered the following facts. He was forty-five, parents dead, no children of his own, and he was "all washed up". He'd been physically active as boy and man, loved to be out in the open. He'd enjoyed working on construction sites demonstrating his strength, "showing off with the lads" till he fell off some wonky scaffolding and broke his leg in several places. "Bloody health and safety" meant he could never return to his work. The hefty compensation he was paid meant nothing to him. "Might as well have shot me there and then, put me out of my misery, no bloody use to anybody." The money took him and Mary to Thailand, bought new furniture and a new bathroom, but he barely noticed as he withdrew into bitterness. How much of this was a very serious Depression and how much self-pity and a stubborn refusal to come to terms with his disability? How could I be of use to him if he wouldn't even look at me? I knew how Mary must feel.

Suddenly there was a loud explosion outside, I guessed about fifty metres away. Frank didn't blink. Soon fronds of pale smoke or fumes of some kind floated past our window, shortly followed by two police cars, their sirens wailing. Still no response from Frank, who went on addressing the carpet. Then came a clanging fire engine rattling right past us. It was scary, but, ever professional, I stayed glued to my seat waiting for the surgery's fire alarm to go off as it surely must. I realised I would have to physically wrench Frank from his seat. He had heard nothing, so entirely dead was he to the outside world, completely entombed in his rumination. The diagnosis was now very clear indeed. Urgent intervention was required.

(By the way, the alarm never went off. A gas canister had blown up at the local pub. A couple of people were treated in hospital but the fire never reached us.)

The doctor and Mary agreed she would threaten to leave him if he didn't at least try the pills. Or she might hint at a worse outcome, being sectioned and given ECT, only to return to an empty house. Surely the pills and the sweet old lady counsellor was the preferred option?

Three weeks later, now on the highest dose of SSRI's, Frank was at least able to meet my eyes and talk about his loneliness and sadness now he'd lost all his mates and his capacity to work. Maybe the time had come to finish himself off, he said; he was just in everyone's way, it'd be doing them a favour. But how would Mary cope? At last, at *last*, someone else was allowed into his self-obsessed universe! The grim tide was turning.

I felt encouraged until Mary called the surgery one day to report he had tried to kill himself with his razor but she'd caught him at it. It turned out that "the last straw", as he put it, was that he'd lost his ability to keep his erection going. There was no point at all to life now, this was proof. Unfortunately the doctor had deliberately withheld from him the fact that one side effect of the otherwise successful antidepressant he'd prescribed was erectile difficulty. He'd seen no point in adding to Frank's problems, and anyway Mary might be grateful for a reduction in her husband's sexual neediness.

The drug was changed and Frank was relieved and amazed to have his potency restored. He made steady progress and by our tenth session showed no further sign of suicidal intent. Mary told the doctor things were improving at home.

Discussion

We see here several aspects of the Depressions noted in previous chapters. Frank was in his early midlife phase but had had no time to come to terms with it before his leg was crushed and he lost all hope of any future fulfilment. He hated his now imperfect Self and the world that had treated him so cruelly, though by the time I saw him his hatred had wearied him: he sounded like a worn out record. His childhood was uneventful but seemingly happy. Sadly he had neither living family to fall back on when he lost the leg nor the work mates he'd so valued over the years. A few wanted to see him after the accident but he felt he wasn't "a proper bloke" any more, scorned their pity and rejected them. All he had was Mary, to whom at night he clung like a lost child. The search for and support of good personal relationships in the patient's environment is a vital part of the treatment plan, so posed a real problem for us.

The collaborative relationship between Mary and the doctor, our grief work in therapy over the accident, and the pills – despite the error over side effects – all coalesced to enable Frank to re-engage with the life he thought had ended. His first major step was letting Mary hire a personal trainer who specialised in disability. "It'll get him out from under my feet," she grinned. What a gem!

Annabel's story

Annabel was fifty-ish, warm and chatty, fashionably dressed and pretty. She ran a successful hair salon, had two grown-up children and a husband she was so preoccupied with I wondered whether he should be attending the counselling appointment rather than her.

"Brian's lovely, you know, good, kind, handsome. Twenty-eight years we've been together. Nerdy though, he's – well – you know, quiet like, reads a lot. Does long distance running, studies diet and stuff, bit of a health freak. No friends, no family, likes to be on his own. What can you expect though, eh? No idea who his parents were. They gave him foster parents. Huh. Perfect in public they were, but behind doors beat him up if he didn't behave posh like them. Made him grovel in gratitude all the time. He hated them. Then he was adopted, but too late by then, just withdrew really. He left school early, just hung about till he met me and we lived in a dump while I trained. Me, I wasn't going to be on benefits forever, was I? No way."

She took a breath and hurried on. "We always had a great sex life though, two smashing kids, flown the nest now. He was a good dad, bit strict, bit old fashioned, but always stuck up for them. He got proper jobs and everything, but, like, well, you know – he never wanted to go anywhere or do anything, talk to anybody, not even me half the time. Me, I love to dress up, go clubbing, loadsa friends. It's been hard, he gets that jealous and sulky when I go out with the girls, though he doesn't say anything, just looks wretched. You can't blame him though, can you? Not with that background. But it's been me who organised all the holidays, dragged him to the movies 'cause I didn't want to go on my own. Never goes to the pub, doesn't drink."

She sighed, looked wistful, then brightened. "Still, he loves fixing up our house, mending things. All he needs really is his DIY and his running and his weird health stuff. Don't get me wrong, I love him to bits, but it's been so. . . so. . . "

"Lonely?"

"Too right. It's even worse now. You'll think I'm awful,
but last year I was horrible to him. I was judging this
big hairstyling competition and there was a party after.
One of the other judges was just so, well, attentive, kind,
thoughtful. We ended up having it off, just the once. I felt
terrible, really terrible. And stupidly I confessed. I thought
it would kill him, or that he'd kill me, he was that betrayed.
I'm his world you see, the only person he's ever trusted in
his life."

Since then Brian had virtually sent her to Coventry, often
eating or sleeping alone, taking even longer runs. She
kept apologising, begging forgiveness, assuring him of her
devotion, never going out in the evenings, cooking his
favourite and fussy food, terrified he would divorce her.
She hated herself for being so selfish, "grabbing my bit of
fun", when she had known all along that the one thing that
would break him would be infidelity.

By now I knew Brian, but what about her? When I asked
her this, her eyes widened and she stared at me like a rabbit
in front of headlights. Her eyes filled with tears and rolled
down her cheeks, unstoppable. "This is what happens if
anybody asks me how I am. Change the subject and I'm
fine, but don't ask after *me*. That's why I'm here to see
you. I can't go on like this. I can't control the tears. All my
regulars at the salon are worried about me, and the new

ones don't come back. It's so embarrassing, even though it only lasts a minute or so before I'm back to normal – gift of the gab, that's me. I'm running out of tissues and can't go on saying it's a cold, can I? People are not stupid."

Ah, I thought, the old "smiling depression". I hadn't seen one for a while.

I asked Annabel to fill me in on her own background. She didn't seem to feel it was that important but she obliged me. Her much loved father had died of an undiagnosed heart condition while still in his thirties, Annabel only six. Her mother never got over his death, leaving Annabel to care for her younger twin brothers, and to a great extent her bereaved mother as well. There was no time for Annabel to do her own grieving as she was too busy coping with the rest of the family, and did so till she left home at eighteen. Is it any wonder she became a carer in her marriage, while choosing a partner who would make her the centre of his universe? A man as wounded and needy as Brian, despite his inability to show his feelings except in the bedroom, would never leave her bereft as her father did. And is it any wonder Brian chose her, an established expert in maternal care and putting others' needs before her own?

I was building a formulation in my mind now, a scaffold on which to build our work together in the short period the surgery allowed. It went something like this: Annabel's persistent conflict within the long marriage was how to fulfil her own, more social needs, as well as her natural desire for more companionship with her husband, without wounding Brian, whose history prevented him from expressing much emotion at all. After almost three decades she'd obtained very little reward for her efforts and sacrifices. Where was her anger and sorrow over this, and where had it been in childhood?

All Annabel could do in our first session was blame herself for that one unfaithful act, which I thought might well have been one of unconscious protest and rebellion, a message to Brian to notice her or lose her, for she'd had enough. It seemed to me that two silently fighting but loving parties in the present, and two long sad histories contributed to these tears that cascaded down Annabel's cheeks whenever she was the centre of attention and could no longer hide behind helping others. I didn't immediately face Annabel with this so far hypothetical model of her rather severe but disguised little 'd' depression, of course. I kept it in mind, awaiting confirmation or negation, while listening each week to what she told me was bothering her at the moment.

At one point she was ready to give up therapy, realising just how deep their unresolved issues were as a couple. She said she knew she had to do this work if she was ever to improve her and Brian's relationship or say goodbye to her father at last; but it was all too much. She was feeling hopeless about the future. "Put all this stuff back in its box and pretend it never happened," she pleaded. "All this talk, all this churning up of stuff, it hurts. Things are never going to get any better so why get myself all upset?"

I felt this was the moment to try antidepressants. We were both surprised at how quickly her optimism returned, though she was under no illusions about the long road ahead. Her present marital difficulty and its links to her unfinished business with both unavailable parents had not changed, but her involuntary tears had stopped as she probed deeper into their cause. Her hope of one day coming to some accommodation with her husband and her past had returned.

Overview: how this talking therapy unfolded

My first aim was to get hold of what we call in the trade the "dynamic formulation", which I've described above. (I have elaborated this concept in my book for counsellors: *The Broad Spectrum Psychotherapist*, Free Association Books.) This refers to the detection of *underlying* psychological conflicts or troubling preoccupations suggested by the client's behaviour, attitude and account of their problem, and constructs hypotheses about how the past may be related to the present. As there were so few sessions on offer, I strove for this formulation in the first meeting, screening out extraneous subsidiary issues, however interesting. Though that formulation was a bit rough and ready, in need of refinement later on as more links were made between emerging pieces of information, it provided a basic model for myself and Annabel to focus on.

Then I needed to think about medication. Annabel was on HRT which had helped with night sweats and hot flushes but not relieved the tearfulness, so perhaps they were not hormonally caused. Before deciding, I would wait and see if the tears lessened when/if we acquired some insight into her problems. Her appreciation of Brian's emotional deprivation already showed she could work with psychological ideas and I didn't want her thinking capacities fogged unnecessarily with drugs, even though any fogging soon clears. It sounds cruel, but she needed her pain to prompt her into facing her long-term marital conflict. If her mood lifted too soon, it would be buried again. And think of the healthy pride she could take in her Self should she manage to get herself well without medication. As it turned out however, the pain was so bad she would have left the therapy. Antidepressants saved the day.

Were ten sessions going to be sufficient if the long-term marital as well as individual difficulties were opened up during the surgery counselling? She would then have to pay for private therapy. I should warn her. Luckily, there was no suicidal risk, no psychosis, and no need to involve family other than possibly Brian. Employers weren't relevant as both partners were self-employed.

Then there was Brian himself. Could he use some help, given his history, and would he want it? Perhaps they were going to need couple sessions later as the marriage had clearly been under strain for years.

The extramarital sex seemed to me the result not the cause of the problems so I did not dwell on it overmuch, given our time constraints.

Discussion

You will have already noted familiar characteristics of the Depressions in both Annabel and Brian's stories: *denial* of Annabel's own needs in order to *avoid* marital conflict that would lead to imagined *loss* or *separation*. Annabel's massive guilt disguised to herself her long-term rage against her husband's chronic withdrawal. The one-night stand, perhaps designed to bring him to his senses and love her as a husband should, failed completely, resulting only in her having to crawl to him even more, begging forgiveness. It proved one humiliation too many and the unshed furious and lonely tears banked up, only to spill over at the least kind enquiry about her well-being.

Annabel's hidden, but very real and rather severe little 'd' depression, beneath her sunny exterior lifted a lot once the chronic anger she never knew she'd been carrying was out in the open, and she allowed herself more compassion toward her own rather than Brian's woundedness.

Brian and Annabel were both lonely people, hungry for the day to day intimacy of marriage yet only able to approach closeness (or snatch it) in the darkness of their bedroom. Each had a frail and doubting relationship with their Self, needing much further exploration, and to that end they both entered separate private therapies after the surgery counselling finished.

Chapter 8

Caring For The Sufferer

With the exception of psychotic Depression, where the previous personality appears temporarily obliterated by the all-encompassing symptoms, these disorders of mood don't eradicate the person's former individuality. In this chapter then, let's look at how different kinds of people relate to their own mild, middling and severe small 'd's; and how their carers, who also have different personalities, deal psychologically with their caring commitments. The way these partnerships are conducted can obstruct or facilitate recovery yet are rarely talked about *as* collaborative or combative duos. Too often the ailment is regarded by partner, parent or family much as would be a bout of 'flu, some sickness the unfortunate individual has contracted from outside, requiring medical and nursing attention that they should passively and gratefully receive in order to get well again. Meanwhile life goes on as before.

In truth though, depending on how it's managed by sufferer and carer(s) alike, a Depression can either cast a blight over an entire family, workplace or marriage, or marshal undreamt-of reserves of love and loyalty among supporters. A Depression is not a sealed off infection, nor the sufferer entirely helpless. Rather does the disorder by its very nature disrupt the usually stable network of relationships or partnership in which it is fixed. Especially when prolonged, a Depression arouses all manner of emotions in carers, from the protectively tender to the most impatient and hostile. Can we take a look at a few examples without judging those involved? These are common observations, not clinical categories or professional labels: you won't find them in any textbook.

Broadly speaking, small 'd' sufferers relate to their condition in a similar way to how they related to the world before the episode occurred. The controller automatically uses the Depression to control others; the stoic puts up with it and rejects help; the needy one uses it for baby gratification; the worrier keeps moment to moment tabs on it and fears its outcome. It can be hard to differentiate illness from personality sometimes. The afflicted person's usual traits – say grumpiness, whininess, pessimism, evasiveness, secrecy, self-negligence, hunger for attention – can become more pronounced as their genuine need for support becomes apparent. They have lost the energy and will to make themselves acceptable to others, to hide or disguise aspects of their personality they formerly guarded and controlled, appreciating how unappealing they were. This often feels to the prime carer that they're taking advantage, or being stubborn, self-obsessed. This may well be the case, but this behaviour or attitude is not calculated: it represents the melding of normal personality quirks with symptoms of an out of order mood.

Equally often the sufferer knows full well the anguish and frustration they cause – they're not dim-witted – and feels even more guilty and self-loathing as a result.

So how much should the main carer discuss with the poorly individual how they are going to relate to each other till things are back to normal? And what rights if any does the carer have to share *their* reaction to having the carer role thrust upon them? Will a family conference to clear the air between and among them all make matters worse or improve things for the duration of the episode? Is the sufferer able to participate in making some realistic agreements with others as to how their temporary indisposition is to be managed, such that the Depression is accorded respect but the carer and other family members are not unduly discommoded? How much responsibility for the effects of the Depression on others can the sufferer be expected to take? How many allowances is it reasonable for everyone else to make for them, and for how long?

Heavens, so many questions! What's the wisest counsel for carers to give sufferers, or should any be given at all? Should the person be kept clean and safe, nursed, so to speak, while the depression itself is largely ignored, left to progress through its inevitable course until the person is back to normal? Or ought the sufferer be facilitated to express his negative mood and darkest thoughts, "let it all hang out"? Or should they be cajoled into "thinking positive", seeing the best in themself and others, looking to the future when all this is over? There's no simple answer to these questions, no rule book. My own view is: when in doubt, ask. Ask the sufferer what they need and want and then say if, when and how you can provide it. And if not, why not. They may have lost hope for the time being, but they still have their reason, intelligence and conscience. Few people enjoy being treated like a helpless child, even if in a Depression they often feel like one. Depressed people still have a functioning brain.

As the darkness starts to lift, perhaps the roles of carer and cared-for can be reviewed. Both parties might derive much comfort and satisfaction from being able to consult, even squabble over things or do deals with each other, designed to regulate the degree and intensity of the caring now recovery has appeared on the horizon. For example the carer might say: "I'll make your favourite curry if you'll get a haircut." The suffering one might offer: "I'll take a turn round the common, if you'll let me sleep till lunch tomorrow without bothering me." The carer again: "If you can manage to have a bath and be civil to Auntie May for half an hour you can stay on your mindless games machine till midnight."

Though they may be unaware of it, and without even doing anything, the prime carer has a critical psychological role throughout the course of the sufferer's Depression. Whether young or old, for an adult weakened by absence of hope the experience of being incapacitated and having to be cared for raps loudly on the door of the vulnerable person's memory store discussed in chapter two. Actual memories may or may not return, but the *low mood* originally occasioned by those stored away events – feelings perhaps of neglect, abandonment, loneliness, rejection – will certainly be brought into the present should the carer's treatment be in any way similar to that of earlier significant carers, thus reinforcing sadness and lack of hope. Similarly, sensitive and loving care somewhat bars the way to old ghosts.

The carer is entitled to their own personality of course; they can't be expected to turn saint, nurse or counsellor overnight. They haven't asked for this position. And quality care comprises so much more than feeding and changing the sheets. Some carers adopt a clinical, almost medical outlook, being faintly disgusted by the self-preoccupied symptoms, the slovenliness and apathy of their charge. Others suffocate the person with attention as if they're complete invalids, relishing their important maternal status. Some actually encourage the negativity of the person (though it's dressed up as sympathy), keeping them low because the caring role reduces their own loneliness or gives them power and purpose that strengthens self-esteem.

In a marital scenario the carer may be keeping a spurious marital harmony going by the way they exercise their role: you don't bite the hand that feeds you. An implied withdrawal of interest and attention keeps the other needy and the carer in a position of control and power. Other couples swap carer and cared-for roles, the Depression changing hands like a hot potato. The covert objective is to bind them to mutual dependence – how else to ward off the heat of denied mutual hostility? Believe it or not, some carers can be spiteful, envying the sufferer who can legitimately demand their time and attention, when they, the carer, would so like it themselves. These are all understandable human responses, almost always subconscious. Recognising them with wry humour rather than self-blame can really help both parties through this unpleasant time.

Some carer pairs, giver and receiver, jointly steer the unwell one toward recovery; sadly others can only be described as gruesome twosomes, even if they do get there in the end. If only we could match up carer to cared-for by their personality traits. The task usually falls to whoever is available or tied to the person by family obligation. Despite doing their best, many carers eventually come into counselling themselves, beset by guilt and resentment. Particularly where chronic and recurrent conditions are concerned, they feel dismayed by the prospect of a curtailed future yet chastise themselves for hating their situation and the one who's causing it.

Giving care

Mr. Smith says to his poorly granddad: "How about a nice hot bath?" ("you stink"). This is fine so long as he can accept a "Leave me alone and stop nagging me" without taking too much umbrage. In a different scenario a mother (carer) might say to her offspring: "You're bringing me down as well, with this endless talk of despair and defeat. Can I have a rest please?" This too is fine, especially if considerately timed, sincere, and without sarcasm or hint of rejection. In fact it shows respect for the suffering person's remaining mental faculties and values; they are not so entirely incapable and frail you have to be on duty for them 24/7. And sometimes a bit of gentle feedback on how they're affecting you can help them muster some restraint and recapture a bit of self-respect in the process.

Making room for the sufferer to regain self-regard is an important part of getting them better. There's a time for indulging, soothing, wrapping in cotton wool, and a time for gradually but supportively withdrawing, much as you would getting a baby to walk. Don't forget that in a Depression healthy pride has been lost and needs reclaiming, not by sugary reassurances but by the rehabilitating person actually doing something for themself when they're ready.

Bear in mind however that their mood state is one of partial eclipse. Often it's only the person closest to them who can judge how much or little the shadow falls and in what direction it's travelling – toward or away from the sun. They are the one best equipped to advise about leaving the sufferer be, versus jogging them along.

Self-care

A really important way to help oneself through this disordered time is by making friends with any antidepressants (this is assuming you need them – not everyone does). All too often just having to take "the wretched things" is seen as feebleness. Should the sufferer develop a vitamin deficiency though, they'd be down at the chemist in no time. This is sheer prejudice arising from that ancient fear of anything smacking of mental illness. We are talking of boosting the circulation of a natural, self-generated brain chemical here, not calling you mad or stupid or weak. There's no shame or criticism involved, except for any that you yourself bring (and where did that come from I wonder?). No one is going to deem the pill-taker unacceptable and exclude them from respectable society. Half of that society has been on them already, appropriately or not. And no need to worry about waking up hooked. Today's antidepressants are not addictive though in the early days there can be unpleasant side effects as the body adjusts.

Alas, some grouchy pill takers hunt down and exaggerate side effects so as to justify stopping them, or complain after only a few days that they're not making any difference. It's as if any improvement has to be the result of their independent heroic efforts. Such a stubborn attitude, misplaced pride though it may be, only works against the prescribing doctor's aims in trying to make them well. Side effects such as tiredness or dizziness usually disappear in time, and lesser ones such as constipation or a bit of weight gain can be dealt with by other means. No one pretends that introducing powerful chemicals into the body is not going to disrupt some of its systems a bit. As to slow results, it can take a month or so before there's any gain (often it's much sooner). Medication needs to be seen as part of the overall treatment plan, not a once and for all sole intervention. It will make its benefits felt faster without sabotage from the very person it's been invented to help.

Meanwhile there are countless self-help booklets available. One frequently recommended by my clients is *Making Peace with Depression* by Sarah Rayner and colleagues (Creative Pumpkin Publishing, 2017).

Whether a Depression hits regularly or strikes whenever that special button is pressed – a relationship breaking up, a sad anniversary, a professional failure – the victim (for so it feels) is wise to prepare for the next assault. What was useful and what was useless last time? How much did they (could they) participate in the treatment plan, keeping hope alive to the very last minute? How was the sapping of energy delayed or slowed down, motivation kept going, till it dried up altogether? When was the right time to stop fighting, surrender to the dark without self-stricture? What point in the mood's progress proved best for counselling and/or drugs?

And how was it afterwards, as the shadow began to slip away? Had the person booked treats in advance to assist their rehabilitation? Had they kept to hand their notes on mindfulness or techniques learned from CBT so as to bolster their recovery? On a more practical but no less important note, had they deputed someone else to fulfil the demands of their job so as to ease their return? Had someone else agreed to manage their finances, fend off unwanted phone calls and unwelcome visitors? Had they arranged for a pal to walk the dog, take it to the vet? Emerging from the dark needs just as much organising and support as disappearing into it and none knows the route better than our casualty. Depressions can't be instantly cured but they can be managed so their negative impact is reduced.

Anticipating and planning for each step of the way themselves enables the affected person to mark their course through their oncoming Depression, feeling terrible but knowing they are moving inexorably toward recovery; knowing too that they haven't simply thrown in the towel, given up. On the contrary, they have collaborated with personal and professional carers, medications where needful, every available bit of information and advice gleaned from reliable sources, and made practical arrangements to ensure they emerge into the light without chaos greeting them (no point in risking relapse is there?). This paragon of preparedness has made maximum use of their central place in the treatment plan, including convalescence.

The interpersonal environment

This chapter and the last considered the treatment, the carer and the survivor themself. The interpersonal environment as a whole often has a strong bearing too. As we've seen, there's rarely one single cause for the condition, though all too often one event or one person is blamed for it! But the human context in which the Depression evolves (the family, family substitute or absence of these) and the care which that particular environment provides or fails to provide is highly relevant to the ailment's course. Does that setting act as a catalyst or inhibitor? Would the Depression have manifested anyway sooner or later? Can well-meaning families and other support agencies be harmful as well as helpful? And exactly when and why does a family crisis become a diagnosable Depression? Think about Bex's story.

Bex's story

Miriam was doing her ironing when she heard noises upstairs. That dodgy boiler again? She'd better investigate. Pushing open the bathroom door she was overcome with a cloud of steam through which she saw her daughter Bex up to her neck in bubble bath, panda-eyed with running mascara, her panties and a torn frilly blouse in a heap on the floor. (Frilly blouse, no uniform? She was supposed to be at school!) As ghastly possibilities sunk in, Miriam grabbed the clothes and pressed them to her nose. Fishy, and there were flecks of blood on the blouse. "Bex, what on *earth*. . . ?"

"Don't tell Dad! Oh Mum, don't tell Dad, please!"

Of course, Dad had to be told. Incandescent with fury he interrogated Bex, demanding to know who the perpetrator was. For God's sake she was fifteen! They must call the police right away. She must see their doctor, be examined. Bex was in tears but refused to go anywhere. She insisted it wasn't rape, would admit only to a date that had "gone a bit wrong". The blood was from briars down by the river, the torn blouse too. About the smell and stiffness of the semen on her clothes she was mute.

Isaac, her father, then tried begging, please oh please let him find and punish her attacker. By now he was crying too, his darling girl so abused, and in broad daylight. "I'll kill him!" he kept repeating. Finally Bex yelled "It wasn't rape, it wasn't!" and fled to her room, followed soon after by Miriam, who tried uselessly to soothe her, while surreptitiously angling for the truth.

From then on Bex remained closeted in her room, eating from a tray left outside the door by Miriam. She could hear her parents downstairs alternately weeping ("how could this happen to us, to our baby?") and arguing ("you let her wear those skirts no bigger than a hankie; you let her paint her face. Dating, she says, dating, at *fifteen!*"). To bring such wretchedness to her parents was almost more than Bex could bear, but still she refused to explain or name the man.

Finding she'd wiped her phone and computer clean of evidence and that her school friends were seemingly ignorant of her whereabouts on that day, a desperate Isaac went to the police without her, but, in the absence of anyone to charge and in view of her refusal, they could do nothing for the moment. The family doctor and a medic friend with a private clinic agreed. An aunt who did charity work for Mind was brought in but Bex refused to talk to her.

The besieged Bex was now becoming ill, barely speaking or eating, not going to school. Isaac and Miriam attributed this to the trauma of the "rape" and begged her (through the bedroom door) to confess all that had happened, so they could put everything right. She was not to worry about skiving off school for a date, she was not to think the attack was her fault: she was an innocent victim. She had to talk to somebody; why not them? Didn't they love her, want only the best for her?

In the end, exhausted and defeated, Bex agreed to see someone so long as they had nothing whatever to do with medicine, the police or the law, her school or the extended family. I fitted the bill on all counts and saw her in my private practice. She would not leave the waiting area and cross into the therapy room until I had sworn an oath not to tell her parents anything without her consent.

She looked worn out, grubby and dreadfully pale. Nonetheless she was attractive and shapely. With make-up and properly dressed she could easily pass for eighteen, which her date had believed her to be. She seemed at pains to be fair to him.

After some preliminary talk about this and that, she decided to trust me and out came the story. It seems she'd had a lifelong close relationship with a distant male cousin, Benji. They'd holidayed with one another's families, been at school together, shared similar interests. At puberty they started "messing about", both curious about sex and masturbation. But as time went on the ever adventurous Bex had got bored with this "amateur fumbling", was devouring contemporary novels ("I'm going to read English at Oxford") and as a result hungered for some real experience. Benji was just like a tame brother, not the real thing, not like in books.

Bex till now had been a confident and ambitious girl full of rosy but anxious notions about her future. "I was so

restless, needed to find out things before your lot ("sorr*ee*")
destroyed the planet altogether – nuke, carbon or plastic,
what's it matter? But I'm not a fool. I'm a feminist, I've read
everything about sex, contraception, male psychology – the
Me Too movement and all that. . ."

She trailed off, then changed the subject. Naturally, she
loved her parents very much, but they and their whole
tribe were dull, too respectable for her taste. This was why
she'd recently been cultivating a secret life of her own that
was so deliberately split off from Isaac and Miriam's that
they could neither be hurt by it, nor given opportunity to
disapprove of her actions and make her life miserable. She
was careful with make-up and clothes around them, did
her homework assiduously, dutifully attended wider family
gatherings. Privately she thrilled to the independent life
she was leading. "I was dying to find a guy who, you know,
would get me as a person but, you know, kind of do it for
me, not like Benji. But I was responsible and careful about
it, honest."

I refrained from comment, so she carried on.

"I did lots of practice runs online, texted and chatted to lots
of weirdos and bores. Honestly, you wouldn't believe some
of them. Finally I found Desmond, final year Life Sciences
at Oxford, non-Jewish, parents even duller than mine. He
sent nice pics – strictly head and shoulders of course. He
was fit all right, lovely hair. We had long discussions about

heavy stuff, politics, religion, all that. Then we arranged to meet up. Daytime I said, local café, cool place where I'd hung out before. Knew I'd be safe there."

They got on well. As they talked, Bex grew more and more sexually interested in this shy, cultured and good mannered young man. There was a heatwave at the time so after their drinks he suggested a riverside walk, which is where she tore her blouse on the brambles. Too hot to go any further, they lay under a tree and after a while he asked her permission to kiss her. Bex "felt all aquiver" and wondered could this be the real thing. He bathed the scratch on her shoulder with river water in his cupped hand and then kissed the tiny wound. Bex was enchanted and responded accordingly.

One thing led to another until the young man's excitement got the better of him. "He suddenly turned animal, a bull or something, snorting and heaving. He went purple, his eyes bulging. He'd left me and gone to some crazy place of his own. I was *nothing*, no one, I was just something he was trying to jab his thing into, tearing at my skirt, my pants. It was horrible, horrible!" She covered her face with her hands, reliving the moment her humanity was stripped away and she became an object, a mere thing. I so wanted to reach out and comfort her, much as Miriam would, but held back. She had come here to deal with her demons and we would finish the job together.

"You'll think me mad, but something happened to me. I *froze*. I was paralysed. I couldn't move. Me, the great feminist, and I couldn't say no! I thought if I just held my breath, let him do what he wanted, it would have to end eventually. If I stayed frozen, made myself be this thing he had to use to get rid of his frenzy, then nothing worse could happen."

Afterwards he'd looked scared, asked her if she was all right, did she want him to go? She said she'd been dumb with shock and just sort of nodded while he beat a hasty retreat, yanking up the designer jeans she had so admired.

The unburdening of her sorry tale afforded Bex much relief, but it was her subsequent Depression, isolated in her room, that now needed our attention. Seeing how her secret life had so dishonoured her in her own eyes and hurt her parents, perhaps alienating them forever, she had descended into self-accusatory reverie. She didn't know, and couldn't care less, whether technically she was still *virgo intacta*; her complete loss of confidence in her own capacity to shape and control her life was much more terrifying. With it had gone every shred of self-respect and healthy pride she had formerly, almost cockily, taken for granted. She hated the way she had entrapped the young man, used him like a guinea pig in her sexual experiment. Surely she deserved the humiliation he'd heaped upon her? Hadn't she asked for it? Now he was being pilloried and pursued for her sins, not his. She felt dirty, spoiled, shoddy. How could she possibly share such thoughts and feelings with her parents, busy worrying about police and doctors and eager for revenge?

Bex's lacerating self-examination, as the lonely, locked away days in her bedroom wore on, sent her spiralling down to very dark places. She began overhauling her life to date, hoping to think her way through to some kind of justification or redemption. She focussed her mind on her lineage, her great grandfather Joel. He was a lowly Lithuanian cook who came to England, married a Manchester maidservant and started a long line of entrepreneurs, her father included, who now owned several hotels. Shame on her, neither of *them* would have messed up at fifteen. She brooded on all those hitherto tedious discussions among her family about assimilation versus retention of Jewish identity. So who was she, with her Jewish parents who observed Shabbat but sent her to an expensive liberal school, with no religion? What about the extravagant bat mitzvah they gave her? Just where did she really belong? What was identity anyway and had she any right to it? She thought long, hard and painfully about the Holocaust, which she had never had the courage to properly face before.

Bex concluded that she'd been so selfishly hungry, so *greedy* for everything life had to offer, that she'd rendered real history, real lives, worthless, tossed them aside if they didn't meet her requirements or if pondering them might cause her discomfort. She hated herself.

All these meditations had been endured alone: there was no one else in her bleak new world who could possibly understand. Till now. Through our conversations, in which she did most of the work, she came to understand that willpower, mastery of information and careful plotting can't command fulfilment into existence. She saw that deceiving and manipulating those who love you doesn't make you happy either. She realised that rescuing the endangered planet rather than grabbing at whatever might be left of it was the more noble plan. She accepted that relations between men and women were more complex and disturbing to her than she had ever thought possible when she'd so believed herself in charge.

Finally, and perhaps most importantly, Bex saw how she had cloaked her fifteen year old Self in an eighteen year old's apparel; not because she was bad, but in order to camouflage and put to the test her muddled desires while assuaging her inadmissible fears beneath an air of self-assurance. All this transpired in what had seemed to her a mad and dying world unresponsive to her needs. She'd been in such a hurry. In allowing herself to assume her actual years, sharing age appropriate hopes and fears with me who would never tell anyone, she came to forgive herself her imagined trespasses, recognising them for what they had been: part and parcel of growing up.

Toward the end of our short therapy she humbly begged to be taken back into the family fold and of course they welcomed her with open arms. Far from time running out she could now experience it as stretching ahead, waiting for her to inhabit rather than dominate it. Her Depression that had hovered between little and big 'D' for weeks was over.

Discussion

The chief instigator of Bex's fall into illness was not the "horrible, horrible" turn the rendezvous on the riverbank had taken, but the shocking loss of her erstwhile confidence, her sudden inability to control events. Without that, who was she? How was she to live? Thus began her self-inflicted philosophical enquiry which was to bring her so low in the first instance, but was to rebuild a wiser Self in the end, one who could understand her mistaken judgements, not persecute herself for them. Unfortunately this necessary and agonising internal journey was not one Miriam and Isaac could comprehend, being so immersed in the more disturbing (to them) matter of sexual assault on a minor who happened to be their daughter. Would you or I have been any different?

Rufus's Story

Rufus was a highly intelligent twenty-one year old with a degenerative illness that was terminal. Doctors had advised he could last another twenty years if he was careful and lucky. Hazel, his mother, was his primary carer and his grandparents up in Edinburgh came down twice a year to help. He had periods when he could walk a little with a stick and others when he was confined to a wheelchair or even his bed. On those occasions he had to be helped with food and the toilet and bathing. He'd given up on antidepressants and the day centre, preferring to study philosophy and comparative religion at home, and to keep a rather literary sounding journal which always remained top secret.

The illness was diagnosed at birth. After three years of trying, Rufus's father admitted he couldn't cope and left, saying he wanted no further contact but arranging monthly payments via his bank for the child's upkeep. Hazel's parents also helped out financially.

Every year from the age of sixteen Rufus would have one or two intervals of Depression bordering on big 'D' which lasted six to eight weeks or so. It was then he came to see me, declaring that nothing could be done for him but he couldn't "dump all this shit" on his devoted mum and it had to go somewhere or he'd go mad. He didn't even have the luxury of killing himself because his mother would never be able to enjoy the freedom he'd granted her. She'd never get over it and would feel that she herself had failed as a mother if her son had so despaired of life. He couldn't win.

Hazel saw a counsellor weekly but the rest of her time was taken up with looking after Rufus and attending hospital appointments. I saw him when needed in his GP's surgery. As a person I greatly admired him. He struggled courageously to find some meaning in his illness and in his life and not to overburden his adored mother. But when his mood suddenly dropped his bitterness knew no bounds. Why has she to put up with him, he demanded? He'd ruined her life, her marriage and now she was so tied to their house she'd never meet anyone else. If she did he'd only be jealous and want to murder the guy: what an awful son he was. Then he'd rage at his cowardly father, furious that he couldn't earn sufficient dosh to send the bastard's money back and tell him where to shove it. He grieved piteously over his twisted body that no one would want, the sexual desires that tortured him. He longed to smash the TV that taunted him with pictures of beautiful people having real lives and loves where he was condemned to watch soft porn and masturbate, which shamed and disgusted him. Everyone thought him a brave and loving person, he said, but underneath he was hating, envious, slimy and dirty, a waste of space. And he hated God after all his reading of every religion known to man, the debates he'd waged online with various scholars and priests. His illness was as random and as callous as the rest of the universe, there was no mystery in it, no meaning. Politics was laughable, no integrity anywhere and anyway how could he possibly change anything in his condition?

These rants left me weighed down and exhausted after his sessions. I felt useless to him. But when each episode was over he would tell me that he'd valued those meetings enormously, for there was nowhere else to release the poison, "no one else who could bear to hear it".

There was no medical or practical solution to Rufus's day to day situation. When mentally well, he struggled on with his philosophical search for some antidote to his nihilism. Except when his sadness became fully fledged Depression and he gave in to despair, he always believed there was meaning somewhere if only he could find it. His mum carried on with counselling, from which she derived comfort and support rather than any insight into her own past – she had quite enough on her plate already thank you. With her and Rufus's permission, her counsellor and I met occasionally to support each other, as we both found the sessions with our respective client very harrowing.

Discussion

This is a sad story but does demonstrate the importance of spreading the load when caring for someone with recurrent symptoms, especially in such tragic circumstances as terminal illness. The main carer needs care, as does the carer of the carers. Counsellors are human and can be overtaken by sadness or even small 'd' themselves when they feel they can't help.

A very important lesson here is that when negative, murderous, hating, self-destructive feelings threaten to break through into awareness, an arena has to be found for them to be expressed, the venom thus drawn from them. *Communicating* mental pain to another, putting words to it and sharing them, is itself beneficial. Pills can't do that.

Like many people having to be cared for when they are very ill, mentally and/or physically, Rufus in fact *cared for his carer* by transporting his "shit" into the therapy room. Many have no such outlet and either unwittingly deplete their carer's ability to look after them by venting their violent feelings, or drive the negativity inward, becoming more ill than ever, or even choose suicide to relieve both parties of intolerable distress.

In this case everyone looked after everyone else and somehow we all survived!

Give sorrow words; the grief that does not speak
Whispers up the o'erwrought heart and bids it break

W. Shakespeare (*Macbeth*)

Chapter 9

Mourning, Melancholy and Depression – Are They all the Same?

If sadness and separation loom large in most of the Depressions, then surely the death of a loved one must bring about the clearest, most extreme example of all? Not so. Mourning and Depression are not interchangeable terms, as I will try to show. Mourning certainly does include an interlude where all hope has gone, but that stage is but a small section of a longer and very natural psychological process, fashioned to ultimately heal.

If unhampered, Nature's methods in this particular regard need no treatment, but sometimes there are complicating factors in a bereavement that leave the mourner buried in the deepest of sorrows, uninterested in ever climbing out. This is *melancholy*, and becomes permanent if left untreated. However long one waits, there are no signs of recovery. In the most serious of cases the person deteriorates into a state of catatonic apathy, usually requiring electroplexy as a life-saving measure. Others may still go about their essential business like an automaton, but their old personality is no longer recognisable; they wear their unresolved grief across their shoulders like a sack of stones they feel no desire to put down.

Melancholy, then, is mourning gone wrong, whereas the loss of hope phase in straightforward mourning is perfectly usual, to be expected. This though is the time the sufferer may toy with suicidal ideas, so discreet observation is needful.

To understand the normal mourning process, we have to fully grasp the concept of human *attachment*, which as many readers will know is the central concept, the lynchpin, in one of the twentieth century's most influential psychologies. In this context attachment doesn't refer simply to ties with people and things that you like; it's much more than personal preference and much greater than affection. It's not the same as love though love may well be in it. Think of Charles Darwin who so demonstrated the fundamental aim of all living species: to survive and reproduce at any cost. *Any*. A helpless infant arriving in a dangerous world must be so fastened to a nurturing source (mother) until they can live independently that both organisms, mother and infant, have to be designed (hard wired) not to wander off, but stay *attached*. Animals are the same; zoologists call it *imprinting*. On TV farming programmes, or walking in the countryside, we watch tiny newborn lambs leaning into their mother for warmth, milk, safety, and feel tender inside: "Ah, isn't that sweet?" What we are experiencing through identification with that nursing pair is the tug of *attachment*. Once we, too, were newborn. This phenomenon is as immutable as it is universal.

The second our umbilical cord was cut we were physically *de*tached from our mother's body wherein we had been comfy, protected and fed, quite automatically. Now we had to draw on our own resources, so turned to the arms, the breast and the warm skin next to us, which welcomed us. Bonding, *attachment*, started. All the same, the severance of that cord was permanent, the route back to the peace of the womb forever blocked. Think on that: *forever.* For the rest of our lives we would more or less look after ourself, but no matter our thrills and spills, successes and failures, we would always be on the lookout for *re-attachment*, a return to that lost paradisical era when we needed do little or nothing to experience total contentment. This search for an ideal second partner can be as painful as it is pleasurable, but nature endows us with sexuality and its accompanying hormones to ensure that between sex and attachment we can't fail to produce a new generation.

So powerful is the innate pull of attachment that social workers gaze in wonder at the child they are taking into care as it howls for the mother who put out their cigarettes on its body. In a war zone that horrifies us as we watch the news, we wonder how starving families in bombed out buildings, surrounded by guns, explosions, daily scenes of human depravity, manage to carry on. Why do they cross the road dodging bullets to find food, still go to school when they might never get home again? Why don't they just surrender to despair? What keeps them going? Answer: their *attachment* to one another. Refugees in their thousands stagger across the dusty plain, arms around their children, their old folk, their babies. They have lost homes, relatives, money, food. What keeps them going when every hope has gone? *Attachment* to one another.

Consider some very different circumstances. A young, clever and talented pop star is rich, well fed, surrounded by admirers, adoring fans. They can buy a yacht, two yachts if they want, obtain sex, drugs, travel, anything they like. They kill themself. For heaven's sake, why? Answer: lots of human contact but no *attachments*.

Cohabiting with a loved one whose attachment to you is as strong as yours to them is the happiest of aspirations, though fulfilling it can be so fraught that many circumvent it or substitute it with other commitments, some adaptive and some self-destructive. Imagine then, having found and enjoyed a mutual attachment in this primordial sense, it's snatched from you by death. Another *forever*. The work – yes work – of the mourning period is to slowly *detach* us from the dead beloved, then leave us lingering in a no man's land of Depression awhile, before reconnecting us to the world of social relations, our interests and our work. Space and opportunity is created for new attachments one day, or for making a satisfying life alone.

Detaching is not the same as forgetting or devaluing the departed one, but the mourner gradually disinvests in those bonds that made them a couple, becomes a separate individual once more. Mourning is complete when dead ones are remembered, sometimes with a smile, sometimes with a fleeting sadness, but in the end without pain.

One can also be *attached to* (not just interested in or friendly with) other relatives of course, or to pets, causes or religions, sometimes even inanimate objects (particularly in people on the autistic spectrum). Once it's happened, attachment as opposed to love or affection can't tolerate a change of mind, or be dissolved by persuasion, logic, or something better coming along. Only Nature's mourning process can weaken its force.

The stages of mourning

The stages of mourning are not tidily sequential. Different people remain in one stage longer than others. Mourners move forwards and backwards between phases throughout the disinvesting process. Take the common situation of a wife losing a husband.

First there is **shock**. Mrs. Jones doesn't, can't, believe it. The news simply refuses to penetrate. She goes over and over what she's been told. Did she dream it? Were they lying? Could there be some mistake? Sometimes panic ensues: I must find him. At once! Where is he? What's really happened? Tell me, show me!

As the fact of death is at least superficially accepted, deeper layers of the attached mind move into **denial**. Mr. Jones is still expected home at five thirty. Mrs. Jones puts out two plates before she remembers. In the supermarket she sees her husband in another aisle, but on closer inspection it's only the other man's posture, his chin or shoulders that bear any resemblance. Feeding the cat, she turns to Mr. Jones to point out the torn ear: he's been fighting that mangy tabby again. Then she realises he's not there.

Eventually the mind allows the terrible loss to fully register and **grief** sets in. It's been described in countless ways, but always it's a state of mental anguish, a wringing of the mind embodied in paintings and plays as wringing of the hands. Some say it's like being on the rack, some that it's being pierced by a thousand arrows. Some literally vomit up the unbearable pain, others wail and shriek. Yet others try to kill the pain with alcohol or aggressive sex or walking the streets till they collapse with exhaustion. Grief, the full facing of loss, is a frightful ordeal but, until it's somehow expressed rather than held in, the person will never be able to *detach* and weave unsteadily back toward their separate Self.

During or after grief comes **anger**. Why is this happening to me? It's not fair, it's not fair! Why take my husband, a good man, when so many other rogues are permitted to live? Someone is to blame; the hospital, his boss who overworked him, the uncaring kids he worried over. It shouldn't have happened. Someone ought to have stopped it. They can put a man on the moon but can't see an artery ready to burst. Fools, they're all fools!

And there's anger too at Mr. Jones himself, for abandoning her when he knows (oh heavens, *knew*) she relied on him utterly. The world is now a cold, hostile place, and he's not here to help her deal with it. With the anger comes **fear** as settled belief systems are thrown into the air. Justice, decency, fairness are all turned topsy turvy if such an unthinkable calamity can be allowed to happen. Many question their faith at this time, just when they need it most. Friends and colleagues rally round but they're not him, they're not *attached*. The dread of loneliness can be overwhelming. There's dread too at even the most basic, practical level. Can she do the jobs and plan the plans that used to be her husband's? Two roles to occupy instead of one. Does she have the energy, the courage, the abilities? Does she even have the desire?

Now **Depression** is setting in, not a discrete entity in and of itself, but one of a series of normal mood changes in the mourning process. Mrs. Jones is no longer completely *attached*; indeed has begun to contemplate her own future, however grim; yet she hasn't yet reunited with her pre-marital Self either. She's finally beginning to absorb and accept that she will never again see her husband on this earth. She can't go back and she can't or doesn't want to go forward.

She broods, doesn't want to see anybody. Is there any point in carrying on without her other half? Her friends have started saying that life must go on, but why must it? She had given over so much of her very essence to Mr. Jones through thirty years of marriage that most of her has gone ahead with him. There's precious little left. This is the time of mourning crisis. She's not aware of it but a decision to live, die or fall into irresolvable melancholy (a living death) is taking place inside her.

This necessity to reclaim parts of the Self that have been deposited into the loved one is what the textbooks call **withdrawal of projections** and is essential for the recovery from this period of Depression. The partner left behind feels empty and without hope till they have taken back all that belongs to them, which in truth was only ever donated on loan. They must redeem what they had formerly and so happily bequeathed to their spouse if they are to live independently once more.

Mrs. Jones may have let her husband make her appointments with the dentist, do her tax forms, make her morning tea. She happily surrendered up a chunk of her self-care to him, enjoyed being fussed over. Now he is dead, she will have to re-own these skills and learn to rely on herself. Can she do that after thirty years? Does she even want to?

This is but a tiny illustration, for wives and husbands project all manner of bigger attitudes and expectations into each other too. One may do the work of being assertive for the more gentle other; one may carry competitiveness for both, so the other can feel more comfortable being the peacemaker; one may adopt sociability on the other's behalf so the shy one can remain in the background. When the partner dies these undeveloped qualities in the bereaved have to be repossessed, and many quake at the prospect. For if they'd been proficient in these areas themselves they would never have plonked them in their partner's lap in the first place. When a partner dies the other party is deprived not only of a loved one, but of many attributes needed for day to day living, leaving them feeling inadequate, exposed and afraid.

The concluding stage is that of **acceptance**, the bidding of a farewell more final than the ritualised one at the graveside or crematorium. Emotions then had to be censored or controlled for reasons of social acceptability and to ensure the caterers and undertakers did their job: weepings and wailings would never do. The organising of the funeral served the useful purpose of distracting the bereaved from all those raw, chaotic or bewildered and empty reactions that characterise the very beginning of the mourning process. But now the tranquil time of sadness yet happy recall has arrived. Mrs. Jones looks at photo albums, concert programmes, retraces favourite walks; not this time pretending her husband is still there, but using them to help her let go of the ties that once bound her. Quiet assent fills the space earlier colonised by rage, fear and unrealisable longings to re-inhabit the past. The marital books have been put in order. It's time for mind and heart to rest, to make the last goodbye.

Three disparate mournings

Mark's loss

I worked professionally with Annie for many years after training with her at the same institute, so I followed the fortunes of her little family with affectionate interest. She and her husband became friends and I first met their autistic son Mark when he was about six. Apart from a slight turn in one eye he looked just like any other child, but he was a real handful. His frustration at not being able to communicate properly was self-evident, his behaviour tantrums very frightening. Sometimes he went rigid and held his breath for alarming periods and at others would turn puce with rage and violently attack the furniture. He was also very curious and physically active, often accidentally endangering himself and his little sister. He was brilliant with card tricks and mental arithmetic that fascinated everyone, but the experts said these gifts would never amount to anything that could land him a job.

Annie made use of every service on offer, NHS and private, consulted every expert and every text book she could find. With some reservation, various drugs were tried but never really tolerated well. Poor Annie was almost at her wits' end when she discovered a charity that trained dogs with the express purpose of calming people who for whatever reason were mentally agitated or distressed.

Mark fell in love, more than in love: he grew so *attached* to his dog Gypsy that his behaviour problems vastly improved. His frustration all but disappeared such that his concentration increased, facilitating his ability to learn, comprehend and converse. Annie quipped they should have called the dog Valium, because of its calming effect on Mark. He now dedicated all his time to talking, feeding, caring for the animal, with whom he developed a language known only to them both. "They're like two old geezers in the pub, nodding away and putting the world to rights," said Annie, inviting me to visit and witness the metamorphosis for myself. I did, and was moved and impressed.

Tragically, four years later Gypsy was diagnosed with an inoperable brain tumour and had to be put to sleep. Annie, her husband and the vet decided to tell Mark that Gypsy was to have a brain operation and then stay at the vet's overnight, after which they'd all say the dog died painlessly on the operating table. They steeled themselves for the worst.

Mark took the news with several sombre shakes of the head, remained quiet all day, then carried on as normal, getting Gypsy's food ready, going on their usual trek across the common on his own, carrying Gypsy's lead. He told his day centre pals and leaders she was convalescing in hospital, but was going to be all right. Only Mark's little sister, now seven, tried to get him to see Gypsy had died. He simply ignored her. He was in complete denial.

Then, in the middle of one night, he woke in a roaring rage and was so violent that he had to be sedated for his own and others' safety. He screamed and hit out at his sister, for the first time deliberately assaulting her as she tried to calm him, gently explaining that Gypsy was at peace, but was never coming back. He just could not hear this. Until now he'd walked out of the room if anyone so much as mentioned the dog's name.

Afterwards Mark subsided into an inertia more frightening to Annie than his anger. He refused to attend the day centre or eat properly, or leave the house. He wouldn't shower or comb his hair and started to dribble (could this have been a variation of weeping?). This went on for weeks until, with the help of antidepressants and a tranquiliser secreted in his cereal, he went back to the day centre, squatting in a corner and building elaborate contraptions with Lego but not communicating with anyone.

At home no one dare mention dogs or anything pertaining to them. Occasionally one appeared on television or barked in the street and Mark would punch the air aggressively and shout: "She died, the fucker, she died!" It was an accusation, as if Gypsy had done it on purpose to spite him.

Almost a year after Gypsy's demise, another youngster's granny was visiting the day centre. Not knowing the back story, she brought in a frisky six week old puppy that all the kids instantly adored and wanted to play with. Mark brooded in the corner with his Lego, from time to time eyeing all the larking about suspiciously. But by the end of the day he was tearing round the playroom, the yapping creature nipping at his heels and squealing with delight.

He soon agreed to another trained dog. On cleaning his room shortly after this, Annie found a battered old tin box under his bed. In it she found a broken and slime encrusted old collar, a matchbox with dog hairs in it, and a turd in a sealed plastic bag. Gypsy would never be forgotten. She slipped the box back where it came from. No one would ever know she had discovered it.

I would consider this to be a normal mourning with a healthy outcome.

Beverly's loss

Many years ago I enjoyed the company of a group of pals in the NHS who met up every third Friday of the month at a local wine bar. Several disciplines were represented. None of us were ever close friends; this was a bit of shared fun and relaxation with colleagues associated with the same hospital. We revelled in a good old gossip and some general letting down of hair.

Beverly was a physiotherapist in her mid-forties, married to a rather rich businessman, but who drove a clapped out car, dressed rather drably, and never seemed to go out or on holiday, or have any sort of life at all from what we could see. She was timid, though clear and consistent in her views, could giggle guiltily at some of our less than savoury jokes after we'd all had a glass or two, but never really came out of her shell. She was a bit of a mystery really.

She missed a couple of meetings, no message, so I was delegated to phone and check she was okay. It turned out that her husband had suddenly fallen ill and had died of kidney failure. She said she'd be back when things had quietened down: there was much to do, lawyers, the house and so forth.

We discussed in some anxiety the best way to handle her return after this unexpected tragedy. Our usual jolly japes would not be at all appropriate. But we were in for a surprise.

On the day of her scheduled re-appearance, we arrived to find a "private party" notice on the door. A bucket of champagne and canapés lined the bar, all for us! Beverly, now some three months widowed, wore expensive heels, make-up, painted nails, perfume, a designer suit and a terrific new hairdo. She was wreathed in smiles. What could have caused such a transformation?

I discovered later, as I got to know her better, that her husband, some twenty years older, had been very wealthy indeed and had left everything to her in his will. It wasn't the money that had wrought this change in her though.

Beverly's father had been a world famous surgeon (none of us had known) who had doted on her but whose attitudes to her and his wife made it clear that he was to be the only shining light in the family. They were mere acolytes, privileged to bask in his glow. It never crossed Beverly's mind to court fame or set her sights on any high powered career; she sort of floated into physiotherapy. In any case by the time she was seventeen she had already transferred some of her near worship of her father to that of her older entrepreneur boyfriend, who she soon married.

Having all her life been overshadowed while nonetheless cherished, it was an easy matter to fit in with her husband's requirements for an intelligent but unassuming wife, a competent hostess and secretary, while holding down a respectable job in the revered NHS. She was a real asset.

The marriage was fine until the last few years when austerity struck and her husband grew moody and drank too much, then started to bully and mock her, all signs of cherishing gone.

Unhappy and lonely, Beverly went to a counsellor and started to see how all her abilities and interests had been *voluntarily* given up, deposited in her father then her husband, as if she had no rights to them at all. This realisation shook her to her core. No one but herself had prevented her from doing whatever she chose with her life and soon she'd be coming up for the menopause. She'd better get a move on.

It was around this juncture that her husband became very ill. She nursed him, dutifully attended his every need, feeling both guilty and excited about the freedom that loomed should he die. Shortly before the end he thanked her and told her he'd never stopped loving her, despite his rotten treatment of her in the past few years. Conscious of her own guilt, she readily forgave and there was a reconciliation of sorts.

After his death and the party she threw for us, she resigned from the hospital, set up a research trust for the rare kidney disorder that had killed him, went on a cruise then promptly joined the Labour party. She became a stalwart campaigner and eventually a local MP candidate. She was far too busy and too important to join our Friday get-togethers.

Beverly recouped all her unused qualities that she'd projected into her husband (wrongly assuming she had no gifts of her own) and at last made good use of them, even if in so doing she earned the title of "The Merry Widow" in our Friday circle. Mrs. Jones, mentioned earlier in this chapter, had a much tougher time, not ever needing or desiring to retrieve from Mr. Jones his practical and loving care over her every need. Doing it all herself was going to be a huge undertaking, not nearly so liberating and joyful as Beverly's. No wonder her mourning Depression was so much longer than Beverly's, who in her counselling had already commenced the detachment process.

Caroline's loss

Of Caroline's three children, two had done well, were happily settled in both marriage and jobs. Her first born son however was still missing after fourteen years. Jason had left home and school for no especial reason at sixteen and had contacted his parents less and less as the years wore on. Once he'd been found drugged (heroin), penniless and ill-nourished in a pillbox shelter on the south coast and was psychiatrically assessed. The diagnosis was "borderline personality" which meant little to Caroline and Ted even after their researches and consultations with various specialists. As a child, he had always been a bit odd and uncommunicative, but would suddenly experience bursts of terror (the doctor said it was anxiety) that left him shivering and in need of constant tight hugging from his mother, after which he would avoid her for days, as if ashamed of his desperate need for her. She loved him with all her heart and soul, thought him wounded in some deep part of himself where no one but her could ever hope to reach.

As a teenager Jason made it clear he didn't want anyone to reach him. He became reserved to the point of muteness, this between bouts of drunkenness, staying out all night, truanting from school and getting himself beaten up in fights he wouldn't explain. There was no more hugging and Caroline despaired but refused to give up.

The marriage suffered as she and Ted quarrelled about how best to manage the situation. As the rows over his behaviour got more heated, Jason simply vanished, for years. There was just a four week old card from Singapore once with a sardonic "wish you were here"; an almost illegible goodbye forever note scribbled in pencil – no address, no clue; a South American set of brightly coloured wrist bands arriving in the post some years after the disappearance. Then once, just the once, a brief phone call to say he was fine, not to worry but leave him alone. Caroline wrote down the date and time, his every word, the tone in which he said each of them. She kept all these scraps of hope in what Ted called "that bloody shrine" in a sandalwood box by her bed.

In the early days Ted had tried as hard as Caroline to understand and rescue their son, till one day he told her bluntly that the lad had no desire to be found, was probably mad and certainly addicted. They had done their level best for him but she had to face the fact that he just didn't want to know them. Let it be over. Let him go. Caroline was shocked and horrified, called him a coward and a rotten father and collapsed in tears, utterly betrayed.

Later they tried to make up. But Ted was adamant that a line had to be drawn: Jason was always welcome of course, but the frantic searches – the police and hospitals and missing person charities were heartily sick of them – had to stop. Moreover he was fed up of being shut out from her. They were supposed to be married. He was lonely, damn it. He was fed up sharing her with her constant pining, unrelenting grief, her vain hopes that were not going to materialise in a hundred years of waiting. He wanted his wife back, but she had to face the truth about Jason. Caroline was equally unshakeable: she would never desert her son.

By the end of that year Ted had confessed to an affair with a colleague and offered her a divorce.

Caroline's years of melancholy, her inability to mourn and detach from her son, undermined her marriage and left her doubly bereaved and abandoned. Her last hope was psychotherapy.

Discussion

Here were three deaths, two of them followed by natural healthy mourning, though the Merry Widow's detachment was accelerated by much needed and delayed counselling help. The mourning for Gypsy the dog was much slower, but Mark went through all the normal phases described at the start of the chapter, albeit in an exaggerated way due to his autism. Sadly, Caroline's mourning for Jason was never achieved. Her Depression became so melancholic she was almost as unreachable as her son. Depression featured in all three cases, but in differing degrees, the Merry Widow having unknowingly carried hers for years before her husband's death.

You may find this paperback interesting, but it does have a psychodynamic bias: *The New Black: Mourning, Melancholia and Depression* by Darian Leader, Penguin Books 2009.

Funeral Blues

Stop all the clocks, cut off the telephone,
Prevent the dog from barking with a juicy bone,
Silence the pianos and with muffled drum
Bring out the coffin, let the mourners come.

Let aeroplanes circle moaning overhead
Scribbling on the sky the message 'He is dead.'
Put crepe bows round the white necks of the public doves,
Let the traffic policemen wear black cotton gloves.

He was my North, my South, my East and West,
My working week and my Sunday rest,
My moon, my midnight, my talk, my song;
I thought that love would last forever: I was wrong.

The stars are not wanted now; put out every one,
Pack up the moon and dismantle the sun,
Pour away the ocean and sweep up the wood;
For nothing now can ever come to any good.

W.H. Auden

Chapter 10

Filling in the Gaps

It's customary in the closing sections of a book to pick out and emphasise the main points of what has gone before, to attempt clarification of the more puzzling ideas, while adding details that may be of interest but don't necessarily conform to the approach that's been adopted so far – the exceptions to the rules, as it were. Far be it from me to break with tradition; so I will try here to reiterate central ideas while offering a few fresh comments on some aspects of the Depressions that connect with melancholy, Attachment Theory, Self-Psychology, CBT, and general psychodynamics.

The Depressions

Let's begin by re-stating a core premise: all the Depressions are characterised by the experience of death – the death of hope. You can be more unhappy than you have ever been in your life, without being in a state of 'd' or 'D'. These out-of-the-ordinary mood states that we call "The Depressions" are all characterised by an absence of hope, not based on an objective evaluation or perception, such as the virtual certainty you will never become a football star, but on the subjective reality of *hope not existing at all*. You are biologically alive but feel dead, even when confronted by happy children playing, your loved one coming home to you, winning the lottery. If you don't feel dead you may be unhappy, perhaps desperately so, but you're not in Depression. The many sorts of Depressions, no matter their severity, cause, duration, type, are all linked by this quality of deadness.

I hear you complain: "Either you're dead or alive, you can't be a little bit dead, or medium dead; yet this book claims some attacks leave one sufferer still doing the shopping while another has to be electrocuted back into life!" In Depression it's the *mood* that may be way out of proportion to the individual's life situation, but it's not a disorder of behaviour or the ability to think (cognition). Precisely because the burdened person is *biologically* alive, walking, talking and drawing up a shopping list are still possible, although the chemistry in low mood does affect energy and motivation, so they will be slowed down (except in agitated Depression) and their thoughts overshadowed with negativity.

It might help to think of a lung X-ray, the radiologist clipping it to the light fixture so as to better see the black spot on the otherwise healthy tissue. It shows that the patient is ill but can still breathe, albeit with some strain, because only a part of the organ is necrosed (dead). The good news of course is that, unlike a physical necrosis, the psychological (and chemical) black spot constituting a Depression eventually comes alive again! Certainly a dead person can't move, but our sufferer *experiences* deadness without being actually dead. Recall the reverse situation: the poor soldier who loses a limb but still feels it as being *there*.

When thinking about what causes proneness to these episodes, we should remind ourselves to avoid the easy route of "blaming the parents". Clearly they carry an enormous responsibility if they were cruel or wilfully negligent, but the average parent who loves their children doesn't set out to do damage, rather the contrary. Nevertheless, along with all the good experiences they provide, they may do or say well-intentioned but misguided things, or through force of circumstances have to inflict separation onto their child. Or they act badly out of their own unhealed pains and conflicts resulting from their own formative years. Self-knowledge in this area is the best protection, but sadly this remains one of the few commodities that can't be instantly ordered and delivered. By the time it arrives it's often too late.

Children are tough as well as tender, have busy little minds and lots of heated emotions. They will make their own sense of what is happening in the household – between themselves and their siblings, between themselves and each parent, between themselves and the parental couple as a unit, and between themselves, other family members and their pets (true members of the household). They're working hard to develop a personal orientation to the whole realm of personal relationships and to find a niche within it where they feel safe. Children are programmed to constantly look and learn. All the time they're theory-building, story-making. Their immature notions about love, hate, power, rivalry, cooperation, rebellion, jealousy, kindness, insecurity that they've gleaned at home will be taken forward in their lives outside, there to be tested, reaffirmed or reshaped by new experiences. But the template has already been laid down. It can be modified but is impossible to eliminate completely, so firmly lodged is it in the deepest recesses of that memory store.

We adults have no power over how the youngster interprets then converts the early external world of family into their own interior model of how relationships work. This is their exclusive and personal construction. All we can hope to do is provide the best materials for them to use in their building operations. Children are not just passive recipients of what is done to them, be this good or bad. As most parents will attest, children have minds of their own and, if they choose, can participate quite vigorously in organising or disrupting family life.

There is no doubt however – and we should never, ever forget it – that adults have an unfair advantage over their children; not only because of their authority over them, but because their own biological/social/sexual/linguistic/ conceptual/moral development has been completed and their child's has not. Society might do a better job of child rearing if its experts concentrated their energies on assisting parents with their responsibility for child development in these very areas. This would be much more productive and beneficial to children than reproaching their carers for being less than ideal. Personally, I've never met a perfect parent and doubt I ever shall.

Atypical Melancholy

The usual portrait of the melancholic is someone disabled by sorrow and self-loathing, morose, preoccupied with some private tragedy, even hospitalised. They could be street cleaners or millionaires, illiterates or great poets; for no one has the monopoly on melancholy, it's just that artists are good at expressing it. Pop lyricists don't do a bad job either. However, melancholy is frequently missed when the outward signs don't conform to this woeful stereotype. A melancholic can appear participative, competent and behaviourally speaking pretty normal, but inside them the mourning process has halted somewhere in its middle and then remained fixed. Ghosts abide within these people, granting no peace. Heathcliff can't let Cathy go until decades later, when restlessly striding the moors in drenching rain he tears aside her coffin lid to lie with her before returning home to die, his face (according to his servant) expressing ecstatic union. Queen Victoria abandoned her public appearances for years, draping herself head to toe in black, refusing to let go of Prince Albert. Put another way, most of her had already gone ahead with him. Both these famous personages nominally functioned after their bereavement but never detached from their lover. There is no "moving on" for such as these.

Every mourner has eventually to choose between killing their dead or dying with them. The successful mourner elects the former, the melancholic dies with the dead. In so doing some are outwardly serene, giving the impression their mourning is complete when, in fact, having already internally died, they are calmly planning a most logical suicide.

Some melancholics remain active but become embittered, like Miss Havisham in Dickens' *Great Expectations*. Jilted donkey's years ago, she still wears her wedding dress, presiding every day over the mouldering wedding feast laid out before her in her decaying mansion. She has stopped time, is dead inside, yet lives on biologically to wreak her warped revenge by poisoning her adopted daughter against all men. It can be hard to see a bitter and hating person as melancholic and deserving of our compassion, but if the definition of that condition is a state of protracted unresolved mourning, then this literary ogress qualifies. Miss Havisham is fiction. Linda was real.

Linda's melancholy

Linda, mid-forties, tastefully dressed, businesslike, but perplexed, came to see me saying she had a good life that many would envy, but for the past few months she'd been waking most mornings with feelings of pointlessness, wondering why she bothered going on; it all seemed a fake, a lie. As the day wore on she'd get too busy with her domestic and charity matters to indulge these feelings and would decide she'd just been silly, she should pull herself together. She'd really tried to ignore these moods, but recently actual plans for suicide were beginning to go round and round in her head as well, till about ten or eleven o'clock in the morning. "It's like a nagging voice, tempting me to do it. Later in the day, like now, I'm fine. Am I going mad or what?"

Linda had had an awful start by anyone's standards. She grew up in a rough dockland area; both parents were alcoholics. They fought savagely and often physically with each other but stayed together nonetheless. Linda and her younger brother watched in fear and dismay. Regular food, clean clothes or plumbing that worked were totally foreign to them. When she was seven both children were taken into care, fostered, and eventually adopted by "decent ordinary folk" with whom Linda "rubbed along" but clearly never really *attached* to, though her brother flourished.

Linda was convinced her brother was their favourite, though the adoptive parents made no observable distinctions between them. Her brother grabbed all the love and attention he could, while she turned inward, cool but polite toward them, gratefully accepting their material care, but resisting any kisses and cuddles. It took some time in the therapy for Linda to be able to recall her secret fantasies during that time. She dreamt of a rosy future, contented babies who adored her, a beautiful home, a devoted husband, a circle of cultured friends. Everything was clean and shining, the opposite of her own first family, which in therapy she scorned and ridiculed, looking down on them with absolute contempt and disgust.

I began to see how she had marked time under her adoptive parents, put herself in chrysalis form, the better to emerge as a butterfly once she had married, had children and a home of her own. Such a life would annihilate and replace her original one, so avoiding the necessity of confronting her loneliness and grief. Her hatred of those "gross and ignorant" parents insulated her from the pain she'd have to go through if she ever faced her ravening hunger for their love, and her sorrow at the endless disappointments. "Who would ever want love from those animals?" she would protest angrily. She was intent on stoking her hatred to protect her from the feelings of loss and abandonment that lay beneath, emotions that might have enabled her to begin the detachment process.

She'd now acquired her lovely home, a kind husband, a good income and social life, but her two teenage children remained problematic. Months into therapy she was able to access and articulate the truth about her feelings for them most of the time. She hated them, and hated herself for hating them. She had been a dutiful, indeed, punctilious mother, but neither son had ever shown any real gratitude or love. In fact each had rebelled in their different ways, one with regular hostility and rejection; the other by a pronounced avoidance of contact, school refusal, disreputable friends. How could they do this to her?

Linda was so driven by her need to fit the boys into her childhood fantasy that she'd scarcely been able to empathise with them at all. So glued was she to her own shoes, she was unable to stand in theirs. It was all so unfair, she railed. Hadn't she given them everything that she had never had, and more? Wasn't it all for their own good? Her bewilderment had made her try harder: she *must* prove herself a good mother, the antithesis of her own. She'd tried so hard to teach, cajole and control her boys into being her angelic ideal, but they'd refused to fit the profile. Over the years, as her husband sided more and more with their children, she'd become embittered, hating them for their ingratitude, their dirty habits, sloppy language, scruffy clothes, their rudeness (shades of her parents?). Why did they so humiliate her, refuse to co-operate?

As all these avoided and denied passions surfaced in therapy, Linda's self-destructive impulses started to make some sense to her, but made her despise herself too. Was she evil to feel this way about her own flesh and blood? Was she no better than her loathsome parents? For a time her mornings became even more suicidal.

Discussion

Should we condemn Linda for hating her children? After all, a mother's remit is to be there for her children no matter what, not the other way round. But such unconditional love had never been shown to Linda, so how could she be expected to find it in herself?

What's happened here? In spite of new opportunities afforded by her adoption, the trauma induced by her biological parents didn't allow Linda to trust adults again. For years her capacity to reattach remained frozen until she could grow up and become the one in charge rather than the one abused, the one who could make life beautiful and safe, rather than vile and cruel, the one who could design, implement and maintain the ideal family, redeem her shame and show the world her true worth. But encasing herself in ice meant that she remained *attached* to her mother and father and the horrors of her early years (you don't only attach to nice people: you don't have that choice at birth). When the time came at last to realise the dream that had sustained her for all those years in self-imposed exile, she met with failure as her husband and sons increasingly resisted her emotional control. Despite fifteen years of heroic effort, nothing had changed. She was still alone in a hostile universe. Those years of melancholy, of carrying around so much sad, unfinished business had served no purpose. Is it any wonder suicide seemed a tantalising escape?

In order to be well, Linda needed a genuine mourning for her terrible early years, rather than rubbing them out, avoiding the pain with a substitute plan. She needed to face her sadness, yearning, fury and grief about her first family, as well as for all the later chances she lost or refused due to her understandable lack of trust. Could she ever learn to care for that damaged little girl inside her with her therapist, rather than foisting the job of mending her brokenness onto her children?

Linda saw herself as a very moral person, so would she be able to bear the guilt if she saw how she had so neglected her sons' needs in trying to meet her own? For the moment she raged and despaired at her husband and children's wrecking of her dream, but could she one day come to understand that she needed to kill the dream *herself* and live, rather than die with it through suicide?

Therapeutic schools of thought: basic models

Philosophically and ethically the various schools of therapy blend into one another round their edges, influence one another, borrow from one another. They're not unassailable fortresses, enemies or rivals – or shouldn't be, though die hard ideologues do still exist. But that's not to say they're all the same so it doesn't matter whom you consult. Far from it. Readers who want their or their loved one's Depressions attended to are entitled to know what distinguishes one therapy from another, so they can choose who to see.

Psychodynamic

You will have noticed by now that my own approach entails the therapeutic pair taking much time to probe into, quarry, fathom what the client's story really means. It uncovers all manner of frequently upsetting conflicts and desires of which the sufferer is only partially or often totally unaware until they start therapeutic exploration. (It should also go on record that hidden joys, attainable hopes and creative talents may be released as well!) The overarching term for this outlook is "psychodynamic". It isn't for the faint-hearted and can be time-consuming and expensive. It concerns itself with what I call the "the behindness of things", referred to in training manuals and learned tomes as the Unconscious, sadly a much misunderstood and for some people scary or downright unbelievable term.

CBT (Cognitive Behavioural Therapy)

Whereas psychodynamic work paddles about in undercurrents, linking past to present, CBT skates very much on the surface and in present time rather than the past. The therapist is not interested in the historical determinants of any Depression presented, so much as how it manifests, what faulty thinking and acting habits are involved and how these variables might be manipulated to stop them getting a stranglehold. CBT is about the precise *identification, management* and *challenging* of problem-causing behaviours and thoughts, psychodynamics about understanding the *meaning* of them.

You may wish to sample some techniques in this paperback: *The CBT Handbook: A Comprehensive Guide to using CBT to Overcome Depression, Anxiety, Stress, Low Self Esteem and Anger.* Published by Robinson 2015.

Wait a moment. If one of the main features of the Depressions is absence of motivation and a sense of deadness, surely any desire to study, gain deeper insight into the low mood or train yourself to manage its symptoms, is lost? True. Any therapeutic intervention can fail if mistimed, no matter its theoretical stance. It needs doing when the unwell person still retains some degree of hope and motivation going into the episode, or is gradually regaining it, however haphazardly, after the worst is over.

But what if the "the worst" won't budge, seems stuck for a prolonged period, neither improving nor deteriorating? This is where the *medical model* can really be of use, is sometimes lifesaving. The right medication can facilitate a resurgence of hope and energy, however small, that mobilises the person to at least try to make use of other help on offer.

The medical model

The so called "medical model" of intervention concentrates on that which is regarded as pathological or abnormal, and aims to target and cure it with a specific agent, usually a drug. Rather than "meaning" or "management" the medical model is aimed at *restoration,* a return to your old symptom-free life. This is as effective as police tear-gassing a bunch of angry protesters who are about to lose control. It disperses them alright, but fails to tackle the underlying causes of the unrest: the protest will surely come again. But that's no excuse for refusing antidepressants when they're really needed.

The Depressions incur a loss of belief in life, sometimes loss of the desire to live at all; so in order to help the sufferer grow a sturdier, more wholesome outlook we may need to facilitate their exploration and review of very deep matters – what goals and attitudes they are going to develop or abandon, what life and relationships are going to mean to them from now on, what their revised philosophy of life has become now they have come through their ordeal. Sometime a serious Depression changes an individual's life forever, for the better or for the worse, so opportunity for them to appraise the experience needs to be available. Medical thinking, however valuable it was in emergency, can't help at this level.

Attachment Theory

Just as the Depressions vary in type, depth and mutability, so does attachment take on different hues. We don't all respond to our attachment figures and/or their threatened loss in the same way. Our personal blend of attachment modalities has also to confront and often negotiate with that of any person we going to attach to! It's a complicated business.

Why, when we crave love and have lots of love to give, do our relationships so often go wrong? Well, we tend to perceive ourselves as empty jugs waiting to be filled with love from another in order to be happy; but we forget that our jug – and theirs! – is lined by the residues of former attachments, *especially the first ones* as babies and children. Our recognition of these left-over positive and negative experiences each time they're stirred up by new possible or actual attachment figures can go a long way to keeping that jug from cracking, or even shattering.

Attachment Theory focuses on how individuals react to the demands and pressures of being in profound connectedness with someone or something. They could be trying to extricate themselves from an attachment but finding it impossible to separate, but more commonly they desire to be at one with that person, ideology, career, art work or whatever it is. However, the wish for a personally tailored commitment in return throws up problems as well as gratifications. For should the person you're attached to wilfully or accidentally frustrate you when you desire closeness, you unthinkingly resort to old patterns of behaviour learned in infancy and beyond, when the people you depended on then met or denied your need. No attachment figure can be there for you all the time, meeting your every wish for intimacy, so disappointment is as inevitable now as it was way back in history. As an infant, toddler, then growing child, you developed methods of coping with these frustrations, and it's these "solutions" that reappear when your present attachment figure fails to deliver. (Perhaps they're otherwise engaged, trying to get their own needs met by you!)

This is a book for readers wanting to understand more about the Depressions, not an academic treatise on psychotherapeutic theory, so I will have to be criminally reductive in summarising these ideas. There are basically five "styles" of what seem like knee-jerk responses to any threat to the attachment itself, any fear of the partner's devotion wavering. They are: secure attachment behaviours, insecure/avoidant, insecure/anxious, insecure/ambivalent and insecure/disorganised attachment behaviours. Each category has been refined and re-refined again by subsequent researchers. What follows therefore is but an overall sketch. There is a great deal of information on the web.

We'll take the human co-habiting couple as our illustration, though we attach to institutions and ideologies too, hoping against hope they'll produce the goods exactly when we need them. Before you decide which style might be yours, do be aware that they describe behaviour patterns not personalities, and they represent only one of many ways to interpret couple interaction. It's important to remember too that a person regularly exhibiting one set of behaviours doesn't mean they can't display others in new or unusual circumstances.

From the psychodynamic perspective, studying the *antecedents* of attachment behaviours provides just one of many useful lenses when trying to understand a person's troubled relationship with their nearest and dearest. From the CBT therapist's point of view the history isn't what counts; it's the characteristic and detailed behaviour that the prevailing pattern requires and into which the client automatically falls given the right stimulus that necessitates inspection and self-vigilance by the client. Thus they gain some control and choice over whether to carry on with the behaviours or find alternatives.

Secure attachment in early life augurs well for later mental health and the capacity for sustaining committed relationships. Even if the child was temporarily left alone when they needed to feel attached, they could tolerate the situation, confident on the basis of repeated experience that their special carer would be back soon. Temporary partings were upsetting of course but the reunion was anticipated with pleasure, not reproach or resentment. Such a child could seek comfort when wanted but self-containment was sometimes preferred; they felt free to choose. It all sounds so ideal, but this fortunate child can grow into someone who finds Depression difficult to understand, having never personally experienced it, so they're not always the easiest or best person to be a carer or counsellor for our sufferer.

Insecure/Avoidant attachment behaviour is demonstrated by someone whose childhood and adolescent experiences have taught them to stay clear of intimacy, which they equate with being controlled or invaded; or they're just frightened of what might be expected of them. They don't reject affection but rarely seek it, and are not too devastated when the relationship breaks up. They can love but don't like to demonstrate it too overtly. However, they are usually loyal, playing the field being too emotionally demanding for them. They dread those three little words: "Can we talk?"

Such a person may be content in their own skin, but if their partner's attachment style is **insecure/anxious** and they're also vulnerable to the Depressions, the avoidant behaviour pattern is experienced by the anxious one as confirmation of their worst fears, as well as a heartless negation of their deepest needs. This insecure/anxious partner sees the avoidance not as a part of their partner's learned coping strategy but as evidence of their own undesirability or unworthiness. They try harder, pushing the avoidant one further away than ever, then give up and fall into one of their lurking Depressions.

Insecure/ambivalent attachment is the push-pull, hot-cold variety. The person in its grip longs for closeness but rejects it, isn't easily reassured though desperately wants reassurance, feels needy but is terrified of dependency. They love their partner but find fault with them so they don't have to feel so reliant on them. They can be alternately aggressive and submissive, depending on what their other half is offering at the time. If some major decision about the relationship is getting close, these contradictory behaviours intensify. The other partner is hard-pressed to work out which bits of the displayed behaviours are due to something they have said or done, so can be put right, and which can be laid at the door of their loved one's intrinsic attachment style, in which case they need not unduly malign themselves.

Insecure/disorganised attachment behaviour (and even the most securely attached infant/grown-up can show this at times) is even more difficult to sort out between two people. What is a perfectly reasonable, understandable way for one offended party to react, given provocation by the other, and what is an automatic retreat by them into old attachment behaviours for which the other can't be held responsible? One wants to go to a hen night and the other had wanted a cosy night in. They sulk and withdraw, complaining it's the second desertion this week. Are they doing their anxious/avoidant number, being too clingy so far as the other is concerned, or are they really being neglected and their complaint is justified?

Quarrels may be unpleasant or ugly while they last, but sometimes a good discussion/debrief after the dust has settled goes a long way to prevent the marital disharmony that builds up over time and can end up in a small 'd' depression (or even spark off a dormant big 'D'). The point isn't that attachment behaviours need correction – too deeply ingrained – but that getting to know each other's stock reactions when attachment needs aren't met improves communication and increases tolerance between the pair.

Disorganised attachment behaviours are an amalgam of all the "insecure" types, and appear whenever someone feels acutely confused, apprehensive or emotionally unsafe. They veer from one set of behaviours to another as if searching for some wreckage to cling to.

Linda, in the case above, is a clear example of how these styles manifest. In her early years she was *ambivalently* attached to the parents who mistreated her in the extreme. She longed for love but her survival depended on learning to hate so as to shield her from the agony of its non-fulfilment. Towards her foster and adoptive parents she was *avoidant* – in truth it could scarcely be classed as attachment at all. As to her sons, whom she saw as extensions of her Self, not separate persons, they aroused in her nothing but *anxiety* and that old familiar hatred when they refused to be clung to and controlled. She played out all these reactions with her husband (*disorganised* attachment), chopping and changing with her level of discontent till in later years his own incomprehension and loyalty to his boys caused him to withdraw from her, which only made her more unhappy. Until therapy she wasn't aware of how consumed she was by her ambition to mastermind a family environment where *secure attachment*, the real basis of her childhood dream, might be possible for her.

You may find this paperback book useful: *A Short Introduction to Attachment and Attachment Disorder* by Colby Pearce. Jessica Kingsley publishers 2016.

Self Psychology

Throughout the last fifty or sixty years in the therapy and counselling movement, the assumption of a reassuring, all-knowing expert dispensing wisdom and advice to the worried and ignorant client has dissipated. It's been replaced with a concept of mutuality, collaboration and sometimes re-enactment (i.e. that which evolves in the therapy room turns out to replicate a relationship issue in the client's real life, past or present and so is ripe for investigation). Nowadays the client is instrumental in the therapeutic endeavour, chewing over with their counsellor what the meanings and relevance might be of the material they have generated by simply talking about what's on their mind in the agenda-less space and time provided.

Along with this change in practice came huge developments in theory. Many counselling and therapy approaches now turned their sights on a growing population of help-seekers who didn't seem to be ill in the conventional sense, but who were more "ill at ease" in their dealings with others and seemed to have been so for most of their lives. Their personality rather than any ailment known to psychiatry was making them unhappy. They wanted to investigate their own nature, not their symptoms. They wished to *be* different, understand how they ticked, not *do* new things or think in a prescribed way. How is a human being supposed to make good relationships with others if they aren't even satisfied with who *they* are? Ever needful of terminology the professionals called this group "personality disorders". Lots of sub categories were added as time wore on, the definitions of which are still being argued over today.

Nowadays Self Psychology thinking permeates just about every school of counselling. It's a standpoint, a viewing platform rather than a set of techniques, rules, and principles. It assumes that for sanity, identity, health and well-being, the human being must generate a Self and then learn to get along with it. It requires constant modifications and growth spurts, honings and mouldings so they *can* live alongside it, whatever trials and tribulations it's subjected to. Only then are they able to extrapolate that successful enterprise to relations with others. This idea in no way contradicts other counselling theories, all of which regard good relationships as critical to mental health. Self Psychology merely (!) goes back to the fundamentals, the need to relate well to the Self before going on to the advanced stuff!

What is this Self that when on bad terms with itself can generate one of the Depressions? To discuss any such idea coherently it's essential to distinguish the grammatical self ("he kicked himself"; "she went to the police herself"; "he did it all by himself"') from *the idea we have constructed of who we are*. We can observe, judge, praise, hate or love that which we regard as our Self. It's the shop window that we present to the world (whatever is going on in the back rooms). It feels awfully lonely when we realise no one is looking in it, horribly rejecting when they're writing graffiti on it, or, good heavens, even crossing the road to avoid it. What's going wrong?

Think of it this way: *The Self is an individual's consciousness of his own being.* Thus there is an ongoing interaction, an actual relationship between the "I" who is observing your Self and the "me" that is being observed, enjoyed, disapproved of or whatever. If you go to a social event you'd dreaded and find, to your surprise, that everyone talks to you, you've chosen the right clothes and have said the right things, you'll return home in a state of happy equilibrium with that Self – no repair required. But what if you are always at loggerheads with that Self, it never shapes up? This is not just about social skills deficits or the odd sartorial error, but about the war of attrition between you and that Self that repeatedly lets you down so that your relationships always go downhill in the end. You're in permanent misery, faced with the alternatives of deeply and honestly inspecting that Self, blaming others for attacking it, or in despair wrecking it with drugs or other destructive activities.

Self Psychology proposes that, whether we are aware of it or not while doing it, we are continuously building, maintaining, repairing or in some way expressing our sense of Self, which as we all know was largely shaped by what we were able to make out of our earliest experiences. This constant attending to our Selfs may sound tiring, but it's a very optimistic idea in that it suggests we can alter and improve that shop window display if we are prepared to go inside and have a poke about. Basic design may have been set up long ago but it wasn't fixed immovably in our infancy, like the colour of our eyes or the shape of our feet.

There's a big difference between selfishness and grandiosity on the one hand and healthy pride – a good relationship with our Self – on the other. If our sense of who we are is fragmented, uncohesed, unlikeable, how can we become unselfconscious and relaxed in the company of others? Does a poor relationship with our Self contribute to the Depressions, or do the Depressions erode our relationship with our Self? If the answer is both, then rehabilitative or even reconstruction work may well be necessary after the episode is technically over. If the emergence from this condition is handled well, it may go some way to preventing or at least shortening another attack.

There's a fuller account of Self Psychology in my 2017 book *The Mature Psychotherapist: Beyond Training and Ideology*, Free Association Books.

Discussion

None of the concepts discussed in this chapter, however assiduously applied, can completely remedy the Depressions. Some combine helpfully for deeper and wider comprehension and therapeutic impact, though it's important not to recruit a counsellor who claims expertise in every therapeutic discipline. At best they could only possess a nodding acquaintance with them all, and, as the saying goes, a little knowledge is a dangerous thing. A thorough training in a core, but non-dogmatic, non-exclusive discipline is essential for optimising a favourable outcome. It goes without saying that the counsellor must have a robust relationship with *their* Self, or you may as well throw all the theory out of the window!

Many argue that the psychodynamic outlook (which includes Attachment Theory and Self Psychology under its umbrella) dwells too much on the why and when of things, on history, when it's now that's hurting; others that it's the only route to a fresh start. Some claim that CBT dwells disproportionately on faulty thinking and bringing people into line with societal norms, so is judgemental and politically dangerous. Others bless their newfound techniques for self-regulation and avoidance of pitfalls. Some say that antidepressants are the devil's sweets, others that they're miracles from heaven. Some say Self Psychology feeds narcissism, others are immensely grateful that their non-symptomatic state and preoccupation with identity is at last taken seriously. Some say Attachment Theory is too schematic and "blames the parents", while others see for the first time how contemporary relationship problems are not always down to them – everyone else has an attachment history too! Can there be any safe and wise combination of all these to suit each client, without diluting the specialist benefits of any one approach?

Loose Ends

The unexamined life is not worth living.

Socrates

The first loose end I want to tie up takes the form of an apology. There may be readers from the LGBTQ+ community, minority immigrant, racial, religious or cultural groups who feel my stories of real (but fictionalised) clients have ignored their specific concerns. There was no intention to leave them out and I understand completely that they experience these disorders of mood just like anyone else, but I used my own practice as the basis for finding the clearest examples of the many concepts involved in the Depressions, and as a result the subjects presented here have been mostly white, straight, and middle class. I trust one day someone will write a book about the political, sociological, ethnic and gender factors that influence the incidence and treatment of the Depressions, and I will be first in the queue to buy it.

Secondly, because my life as a therapist has spanned half a century, many of the stories I've related happened long before gender issues, race and cultural diversity were big talking points. It might also be remembered that often people from minority groups seek therapists from their own background, so my sample of minority group sufferers is in any case rather limited as I am white, straight and I suppose these days "middle class".

Another complaint may be that it's all very well for those who can afford months of private treatment. Why should their stories be granted priority over people from poorer backgrounds? As many readers trying to access psychotherapy in the NHS will know, medium to long term work is virtually unavailable, short term CBT being the government's treatment of choice. This is why many of my stories have had to be taken from my private practice, where there is time to unravel the complexities of a mood disturbance's origins. This of course means you've been reading largely about the Depressions in people who can pay. However, my work in the NHS over many years has taught me that poverty or affluence makes little difference to the subjective suffering of rich and poor alike, only to the treatment available to them, and perhaps the somewhat indiscriminate use of medication in the NHS for want of better provision.

A little recapitulation

I would like to stress once again that little 'd' and big 'D' may differ but they deserve equally serious attention. There's no clean cut-off point between the two, as an untreated little 'd' can morph over time into the major kind. Big 'D' such as bi-polar or uni-polar may descend on the person slowly or overnight and often has an established history and pattern, similar to that of other family members and/or earlier generations. Childhood issues may seem not to have anything to do with the extreme but predictable imbalance of brain chemicals, so what's the point in disinterring ancient history? For the time being we may have to accept that the genetic predisposition to potentially psychotic illness is unalterable. However, many dynamic therapists believe that underlying unresolved historical issues do have a bearing on this illness. When current events lean heavily on the memory store the latent illness can be activated. Whatever the truth of this, counselling support during the recovery phase or in actual remission can be very helpful in the climb back to self-regard and confidence. This is especially so where the person's family is unavailable or too dysfunctional to be of much use.

As to little 'd' I do believe many more sufferers could be helped and recovery speeded up if the unconscious conflicts, poor relations with the Self, and the true function of the depression were identified in a counselling relationship, with or without the additional assistance of medication. Even in preordained cyclothymia, whether the swings amount to illness or not, these other factors are worth investigating and may render the moods less giddying.

In short, no one ideology or set of techniques fits every case and no instant "cure" or antidote exists, while many claim that little 'd' is more of a how-to-live crisis than an illness. (In this regard I would suggest reading Dorothy Rowe's work, especially *Depression: The Way out of your Prison*, Harper Collins 2003.) But whatever plan is alighted on to cope with the episode, human connectedness, be this family, friends or counsellor, is a vital ingredient for its success. When the sufferer's mood drops to its lowest, when nothing anyone says or does makes the slightest dent in their hopelessness, the presence and loyalty of loved ones really counts. As the person looking after them, you may want to run away from the unrelenting misery or shake them into seeing straight or shout at them for not accepting the care you offer. You may want to just weep in exasperation that all your efforts seem futile. But be assured that, however inadequately you feel you have dealt with them, the refusal to abandon them will be absorbed into their system. As the eclipsing shadow moves on and light starts to glimmer, that remembered support will form the very basis of convalescence. They will think, "Even at my worst I was accepted. I counted for something."

A note of caution

The categories little 'd' and big 'D' are convenient shorthand
terms but they each cover a broad range of conditions.
It's not enough to say the difference is simply whether the
person can function day to day or whether they're in total
breakdown. This is too crude a measure for there are so
many stages in between. From the outside someone's state
may seem like little 'd', but for all we know they've been
carrying melancholy for years and are much more ill than
we think. A psychotic postnatal Depression diagnosis may
not be finished when sanity returns. Mum may be far from
recovery, may remain in a little 'd' for months or years till
she is properly better. Little 'd' itself can move from mild
to severe and back again, depending on how much of the
sun is blotted out by the eclipse as shared by Jo (Chapter 6).
Someone with a history of cyclical attacks (uni- or bipolar)
doesn't have to be completely psychotic to qualify for the big
'D'. The person may move in and out of psychosis or hover
on its edge during the course of a single attack.

Labels and categories can be misused. They are not
cast-iron truths, just tools to aid us think about and
discriminate between areas in this vast field, and in so
doing organise better treatment plans. Even so, such
arrangements should be flexible, tailored to the needs of
each individual sufferer, rather than being squeezed into
some pre-existing diagnostic box so we can tell ourselves
we now have the problem under control.

Is there *anything* hopeful in going through a Depression?

No one seeks this awful affliction but nonetheless many claim to have benefited from it. I know of many uni- and bipolar individuals who have for certain periods declined their maintenance medication, so risking their health, career and relationships. They did this because they missed the former richness and colour – including the dark shades – of their extraordinary mood changes. The thoughts and emotions accompanying the highs and lows gave their life meaning and variety, though they dreaded falling prey to the extremes to which their illness sometimes drove them. In order to keep a hold on hope and perhaps to defy Fate, they insisted on casting aside lifesaving drugs for a while. I noticed that those of artistic bent claimed to have done their best work when off drugs and a bit too high or too low for their doctor's comfort, but just at the right level for them to create something really satisfying.

I have worked with countless little to middling 'd' people who bemoan their proclivity to this wretched state but who, having recuperated, rejoice in the insight and maturity brought forth by their personal explorations in psychotherapy. Life is so hectic these days that getting to know, like, and enjoy one's Self tends to be shoved down the priority list, to be replaced by gratifications more instant and pleasurable. So if self-knowledge is a valuable thing, it could be argued that any mood problem that necessitates counselling help is desirable. Indeed I hope some of the stories I've told show that one of the functions of little 'd' is to prompt the person undergoing it to take stock of their lives, for at the moment they may be taking the wrong direction. In that sense little 'd' depression may be regarded as the friend who brings unwelcome news but who all the same needs listening to.

All the Depressions are characterised by temporary deadness (at least of the eclipsed section of the mind) and deadness is the complete absence of hope. What positivity can possibly come from this despair? Leonard Cohen had something wise to say on this subject:

> *Let judges secretly despair of justice: their*
> *verdicts will be more acute.*

> *Let generals secretly despair of triumph;*
> *killing will be defamed.*

> *Let priests secretly despair of faiths; their*
> *compassion will be true.*

He sees that punishing, murdering or rendering evil our unacceptable passions and conflicts always miscarries. For when the moral prohibitions and exhortations we've absorbed from our institutions, leaders and cultural traditions fail to keep our true nature under wraps, we end up persecuting ourselves with guilt, self-hatred, a sense of inadequacy – and maybe psychiatric symptoms! Better surely to accept our less than admirable self-interested impulses for what they are, rather than waste precious energy in trying to wipe them out and kid ourselves we are thus ennobled? If we could redirect our time and efforts from repression into honesty, learn to tolerate and manage our shortcomings rather than deny them, maybe we could then find room for our more honourable side to flourish and achieve great things.

As Oscar Wilde drolly, but astutely, observed:

> *We are all in the gutter, but some of us*
> *are looking at the stars.*

Yes.

POST SCRIPT

COVID-19 and the Depressions

Mr. Khan is a middle aged security guard who lives with his shop assistant wife, his asthmatic and over-anxious mother-in-law, four kids and a dog. They live in a ground floor city flat with a tiny front yard onto a busy street. At the moment he is signed off work with "depression", sitting around doing very little and barely speaking. The radio, which Mrs. Khan keeps on in the kitchen at all times, begins to warn about COVID-19, its terrible effects in China and the likelihood of it arriving in the UK.

Mrs. Khan notices her friends falling into two camps. They are either full of fear, some almost paralysed by it, while others adopt an attitude of airy dismissal: the press are exaggerating as usual and in any case the government will sort it. Mother-in-law buys gallons of disinfectant and as many toilet rolls as she can carry. Mr. Kahn barely reacts to the news; doesn't he always see Armageddon on the horizon anyway?

As pandemic is declared, the death toll rises; first the already sick and elderly, then NHS staff, care workers, healthy adults, teenagers even. Soon one hears of neighbours, distant relatives. Then the prime minister himself. Is no one safe from this deadly virus? There is no vaccine, no cure. Has Hope abandoned us? The tally rises fast. Pubs and restaurants must stop trading. All but key workers must stay indoors. Along with others, Mrs. Kahn's shop closes and she's confined to the house.

The nation is momentarily stunned. This confirmation of the possibility of imminent and random death is rapidly followed by the need for proof – evidence, reiteration of the facts (as described in chapter 9). Has there been some ghastly hoax or a terrible mistake? Some people panic, like Mrs. Khan senior, the chemicals of fear drowning her brain's capacity to think. As "social distancing", "shielding" and "self isolation" become advisory, then compulsory, she finds herself unable to breathe – has she succumbed to the virus? She won't eat, trembles all over as she stares death in the face. But then each day, as the crisis deepens, she discovers to her genuine surprise, that she has survived.

Mrs. Khan senior knows from her GP that chronic anxiety and cleaning rituals represent the constant dread and warding off of some feared disaster. Listening to the ever increasing litany of deaths on the news, it hits her one morning that her years of suffering have been in vain. The catastrophe has happened anyway! She herself could be next: her rituals and self punishments designed to appease the Fates have never been any use at all. So she'd better pull herself together. Her daughter and grandchildren need her, especially now the schools are closed and the yard gate, post box and bins require daily disinfection.

Several of the Khans' acquaintances are enjoying working from home – no early alarms, hectic travel. It's Spring: games in the garden with the kids, nights in, meals and TV with the family instead of members hiving off into their separate social universes. The younger Mrs. Kahn hears that some marriages and parent/child relationships are deteriorating with the enforced intimacy. But others seem to be healing, given the opportunity to spend time together, to really talk, close ranks against the deadly enemy reminding them every day of the preciousness of their ties. The more harassed, incarcerated and envious Mrs. Khan suspects that many have simply screened out the horror of what is occurring throughout the world, and are residing in what readers of this book would call denial (chapter 6). They are almost making a party out of this disaster so they can avoid really dealing with it.

Now in total lockdown, week after claustrophobic week, one might expect terror or despair to stalk the land, the less fortunate and less psychologically defended people jumping off cliffs or overdosing. But no: manic denial comes to the rescue (this "defence" is not value-laden, immoral, weak, or even praiseworthy; it's just one way of coping with overwhelming threat). Out of the nation's collective memory store (chapter 2) emerges the fighting spirit of World War Two, the call to unity, the sinking of differences in a defiant, sometimes reckless drive to organise, organise and organise in the interest of every citizen, sick or well, rich or poor. To survive, we do as they did, generate *attachment* one to another (chapter 10). We become an inter-dependent herd, rather than lone beasts out for our own advantage.

Against all the odds, seemingly overnight, we turn into a nation of valiant volunteers while health professionals, politicians, scientists and computer modellers hectically plan the overall strategy against this invisible foe. What supplies do exist are immediately distributed by unsalaried amateurs, mere foot soldiers (and later by real soldiers), to all in need, prioritising the old, the chronically ill, the housebound. So long as we toil together, day and night, deploying any and all means available, there'll be no time or place to panic, to actually *experience* our fear. We are uncommonly brave, even the most frightened of us; for should one of us weaken it could set off a contagion as dangerous as the virus itself. We must keep busy, manically busy, at all costs.

In the absence of any assurances that we and our loved ones are going to pull through, we seek direction from undisputed Authority. At first our trust is located in the trinity of Prime Minister, Scientific Advisor and Chief Medical Officer. We dread yet long for their daily bulletin, stern but calm parents addressing their scared children. We believe, have to believe, in their limitless power, strength and knowledge. Nurses and doctors are elevated to the status of heroes and saints, though they most of us all, have to daily dispatch bodies to the mortuary, the covered trolleys demonstrating the inescapable truth of their impotence without aid of a vaccine. No matter, we still laud them, our only hope of rescue should we fall ill. Every Thursday at eight p.m. we pour into the streets, join our neighbours (from 2 metres away) in clapping and cheering and the banging of saucepans, as if collectively invoking some supernatural force that might bestow upon the NHS superhuman powers in this, our hour of need. Superstitious maybe, but it keeps up our spirits, while reinforcing that sense of nationwide attachment that reassures each of us that though "isolated" and "socially distanced" we are not alone.

However, these rituals and incantations can't cure a single sufferer in intensive care. Deep in our hearts we, and Mr Kahn, know it.

Mr. Kahn thinks about himself. Consumed by his own individual misery, how much more loathsome, useless and pathetic must he be, to do nothing whilst his whole family join the futile but admirable industry of all those who know they are finished but still refuse to give up Hope. It's a baseless, delusional Hope in his eyes, yet they cling to it still. Why oh why can *he* not feel it? (This absence of

Hope is the base line of all the Depressions – chapter 1)
What he does feel is the shame of not contributing. He
excoriates himself for his self preoccupation and stasis
when all about him others risk their very lives for one
another, be it a food delivery, a supermarket check-out, a
tube train, a laboratory or a hospital.

Mr. Kahn mobilises himself. Heavy hearted but
determined, he encourages the children to adapt to online
tuition, looks after them as his wife collects essential
prescriptions for marooned neighbours. He exercises the
dog for its regulation hour a day, assuring his worried,
self isolating mother-in-law that he'll keep it two meters
from other canines in case of infection. He brings home
her shopping, puts in an hour or two at the food bank.
He is not a changed man now, just a decent one; for a
Depression doesn't kill conscience. Rather is his mood
disorder under lockdown too, not allowed out to bother
or contaminate people until this crisis is over. Will his
mother-in-law's abated anxiety also return, and with the
same intensity or not, once it becomes safe to have panic
attacks again?

Social integration, strong family bonds, a purpose
and meaning to one's day to day actions certainly help
prevent, minimise or manage symptoms of Depression
and associated conditions, but their causes (chapter 2)
are so interweaving and complex that it would be a grave
mistake to call this transient Utopia a cure.

At the time of writing this, the COVID outbreak has just reached its peak and we are daring to consider our future (there might actually be one!) while simultaneously battling with the terrible Now. We are starting to withdraw our idealised projections onto authority figures and ministering angels. Child-like dependency in the face of the malevolent Unknown is giving way to a more collaborative, less defended approach. There's rational appreciation and evaluation of what has been done for and by us so far; but also much criticism of our leaders' shortcomings. There are demands that they magic more Personal Protective Equipment into existence, instantly conjure up funds for those falling through the chancellor's emergency net, issue better statistics with more speed and clearer interpretation, locate millions of testing kits. What's the Exit Plan? This isn't just the clamour of an ungrateful population, but the embryonic stirrings of reality based *acceptance* (chapter 9). The unalterable facts of the recent and current situation are being examined and weighed, as the country struggles to come to terms with the loss of its former illusion of invincibility. All its prideful science, its wealth, its good national governance has proved useless against a microscopic bug. True acceptance is a slow and humbling process intertwined with all the other mourning reactions discussed in chapter 9. Our rehabilitation will require so much more than the rebuilding of the economy.

Once current complaints are resolved, one can predict a

period of pervasive sadness, of emotional deadness even, as we look back at the senseless horrors we have endured and which many of our fellows did not outlive. We will have to confront our helplessness and failure in the face of their desperate need. How are we to live knowing that nothing we do now, not even a vaccine, can bring them back? This is equivalent to the temporary Depression experienced by the bereaved individual in normal times. As restrictions are gradually lifted, sheer relief and the effects of being cooped up will release much pleasure as we superficially re-engage with our social and work life. But for a goodly time yet the shadow of all those unnecessary and pointless deaths – so many deaths – will linger, reminding us of our human frailty and the crucial importance of our personal relationships.

If allowed to take its quiet course and not be corralled by denial, be this quiet or manic, our collective mourning might make us a more compassionate, altruistic country than before. In World War 11, as everyone pulled together, the suicide rate dived. Once society found its feet again, the rate rose, but not to the same degree. Had the horrors of war taught us something? What will happen this time?

Mr. Kahn and his mother-in-law may or may not have to endure the return of their symptoms when all this is over. Will their COVID experience have changed or modified their relationship with their Selfs (chapter 1 and 10) such that they can function better, or when the emergency is concluded and their contribution to the common good is no longer critical, will they relapse? How many others have kept their distress on hold, only to need help more keenly, as soon as the usual health services are resumed? Is the NHS prepared for this?

And what of all those who have seldom, if ever, experienced little or big "D" and its associated syndromes? They are not necessarily immune to the effects of a national emergency.

What of normally hard-headed politicians who have been carrying monumental responsibility for our survival, as well as the burden of a nation's idealised projections and subsequent expectations? Then, later, they have had to absorb furious demands from all sides that they produce instant solutions to intractable problems on which they have already been working night and day. What happens to their mental health when their best is never good enough, yet they cannot, must not, abandon their post? And what if all this awakens feelings of inferiority or inadequacy that tormented them as a child, feelings they thought had been dealt with long ago? High powered public servants don't enjoy special protection from Depression, but where are they to take it? And dare they show it?

What of young and healthy nurses, doctors and paramedics, many with children or aged parents to worry about? Day in day out, flooded with cases, most terminal, there's no time to process each death, no time to comfort shocked and bewildered relatives, let alone themselves and one another. They have to watch victim after victim die alone, unable to breathe, organs fast failing, no family hands to hold. Shipped off smartly, instantly forgotten, their bed is disinfected for the next patient, and then the next. Yet the staff dare not complain or weep or desert the enterprise. Should one crack under the mental pressure of facing so much failure, the whole team will crack: morale is all. When we finally have a vaccine, and healers can once again heal, how much Post Traumatic Stress Disorder are we going to see, rather than unmitigated joy? And will our mental health services be ready for this? We owe the NHS more than a banging saucepan and a rainbow banner in our window.

What of the lonely elderly, those who for the first time in years felt cared for, as milk and medicines were left on the doorstep, or volunteers phoned them for a supportive chat each week, or carers came despite the risk? Many old and lonely citizens felt like proper citizens for once. They were noticed, valued, respected, taken account of. They featured nightly on the news. Later on, many will guiltily recall that during the most terrifying period of our history since the Second World War, they were happy! What is going to happen to them when all this attention is withdrawn? No amount of geriatric antidepressants is going to solve this sudden and damaging deprivation.

What of the volunteers? The simply good hearted will find other causes to serve, but what of those formerly alienated from society – the homeless, the untreated mentally sick, addicts, the unemployable – who found reason to live in serving their own? Should not their efforts be built upon, invested in; recognised as a different and legitimate way to help those often seen as "beyond the pale"?

Then there are all those seemingly happy people, whose good relationship with their Selfs can only be maintained by financial/business/social/professional success. What will the prohibitions and the economic downturn do – or have already done – to them? More importantly perhaps will be the knock-on effect to their families and children should they become Depressed. What of domestic violence, more than usually concealed as COVID kept sufferers and perpetrators indoors for weeks on end? How long will people who've been trapped in potentially murderous situations like this have to wait for an appointment? What of those whose cancer treatment, hip replacements, urgent brain or body scans had of necessity to be curtailed? Which of them can adjust to what looks like a long uncomfortable wait, and which will develop a mood disorder as their physical deterioration, pain and chronic frustration interact with other difficulties that were not major problems before?

Still reeling, and exhausted from trying to manage the immediate consequences of COVID, can our beleaguered government find the wherewithal to see and plan for the massive mental health provision *of a holistic kind* that is going to be needed as the outbreak subsides, especially for the treatment of the Depressions?

Written April 24th 2020.
(The Khans are of course fictitious.)